FACING THE ISSUES 3

WILLIAM J. KRUTZA
AND PHILIP P. DI CICCO

Contemporary
Discussion Series

Baker Book House
Grand Rapids, Michigan 49506

ISBN: 0-8010-5300-5

Copyright 1970
by Baker Book House Company

First printing, August 1970
Second printing, November 1970
Third printing, August 1971
Fourth printing, August 1972
Fifth printing, November 1973
Sixth printing, May 1975
Seventh printing, September 1977
Eighth printing, March 1979

PHOTOLITHOPRINTED BY CUSHING - MALLOY, INC.
ANN ARBOR, MICHIGAN, UNITED STATES OF AMERICA
1979

Introduction

A Christian without Social Concern Is a Misnomer

CHRISTIANS NEED CONSTANT CHALLENGE and stimulation to apply their faith to the current problems of society, otherwise they forget that the gospel meets man's temporal as well as his eternal needs. Jesus Christ still is the answer to man's desperate plight. People need to turn to Him, not only for eternal salvation, but for the inspiration, challenge, and power to live abundantly and productively.

Being a Christian is more than believing doctrines and following rules. It is based upon a vital relationship with Jesus Christ that motivates a person to proper involvement both with God and with men. A Christian without social concern is a misnomer.

God desires us to love and worship Him, but we cannot do this apart from true love and active concern for people. The Bible plainly tells us that love for God motivates a love for men. If we are without love and compassion for men, God's love does not abide in us (I John 3:17). To ignore social concern is to deny our faith. Concern for others is intertwined throughout the fabric of the Bible.

We believe Christians need to aggressively and creatively confront the issues of our day with dynamic, life-changing applications of the message of Christ. Christians must be willing to enter whatever dialog may be necessary to impress the biblical message of hope upon our despairing society.

To do this we need to understand what society is saying, where it stands on issues, and where it is heading. If we fail to listen to what the world is saying and even to its criticisms, we will block any hope of getting the world to listen to us. We need to let the Bible shed its light, even if it becomes an agonizing and painful process. If we do not apply the Bible to today's issues, we cannot expect unbelievers to see the pertinence of our message.

But action must follow talk. It is not enough to propose that we have the right answers. We must back up beliefs with deeds. We are to be doers of the Word. This will require courage when we have faced some issues. We might be forced to put our reputations on the line, either with the world or with those in the church who worship traditions, for what we hold to be the honest approach to both the Scriptures and to the issues.

We should take an active part in community programs on sex education and environmental pollution. We must cooperate with local officials to reduce crime and drug addiction. We must encourage local churches to cooperate with others in welfare and aid programs. We must be willing to speak out on touchy and unpopular issues.

Doing these things doesn't mean that we have forsaken the main thrust of the gospel — personal salvation by faith in Jesus Christ. It is simply carrying out the full implications of the gospel Jesus personally preached and practiced. Concern for others is the natural outgrowth of Christian experience and expression.

The world today usually criticizes the church for its non-involvement. It doesn't really want the gospel's answers because of the basic sinfulness of man that seeks its own remedies and has an aversion to God's truth. But in desperation the world is crying out to the church to do something about our problem-

4

infested culture. It will blame the church for any failure to meet the staggering needs of mankind.

On the whole, the church has not demonstrated to the world that our faith works in the pressured problems of society. We have neatly divided our Christian living into compartments and have failed to show that genuine faith produces genuine concern and action. We have been too slow in involving ourselves in alleviating society's problems. We have been too timid in applying the Bible to social needs. We have failed to show our sincerity to the world and it has lost confidence in our watered-down words. If we believe that "Christ is the answer," we must begin acting like it rather than just saying it!

One way to get started would be to make a list of names of national, state, county, and local officials to whom one can write on any issue that has political implications. The Christian should write, not only stating a position, but offering concrete proposals. Next, the participant should survey his local community, his denomination or independent home mission outreach ministries, and develop personal and local church social involvement goals.

Roll up your sleeves whenever necessary to apply the Christian principles that develop out of these discussions. The kingdom of Christ will be expanded through your efforts.

WILLIAM J. KRUTZA
PHILIP P. DiCICCO
Wheaton, Illinois

How to Have
a Profitable Discussion

LECTURERS MAY FIND A GOLD MINE of helpful material in this book, but it is not intended as source material for lectures on the issues that face Christians today. It is rather intended to excite people to tackle some of the pressing issues of our day. The way this book is put together — first stating what others have already said on the issues, followed by Scripture that applies to the subjects, and then with the "What Do You Say?" section — will create mind-challenging situations in which people can express their views and hopefully come up with genuine Christian application and action. To facilitate this process we offer the following suggestions:

Each participant should have a copy of "Facing the Issues." This will allow for pre-discussion study of the materials and time to do additional research. The more each participant thinks through the materials, the more profitable will his or her contributions be in the discussion sessions.

Keep each discussion centered upon the theme of the materials presented in that particular discussion. A discussion that drifts to subjects unrelated to the theme usually does not accomplish much in the thinking of the participants. Save other topics for future discussions. Possibly have one member of the discussion group take notes on subjects to be discussed at another time. More than ample material is included in each chapter.

Have each member of the group participate in each discussion. It is easy to let one or two people do all the talking, but this may not be of the greatest benefit to those in the discussion group. The discussion leader should guard against this and consciously ask others to voice their opinons or give additional information. Some silent members of the group may have the best ideas to contribute because they have been thinking them through while the others have been talking. All those who have ideas should be allowed to express them before going on to the next question.

Use the printed materials as a guide, not as a needs-to-be-covered curriculum. The material in this book is given as a springboard for constructive discussion. The discussion questions need not be taken in the order given. Nor is it necessary to seek answers to all of the questions. If a question does not fit your particular situation or locale, go to the others or rephrase the question to make it relevant to your situation.

If your group gets wound up on one or two questions, don't insist on going further. Save the remainder of the questions for the next discussion session or for an after-meeting coffee time.

Seek to develop positive, workable solutions to the issues. We already know that the issues are controversial. If they weren't, they would not have been included in this book. Some might be tempted to give quick and easy solutions — often negative ones to the issues in this book. Anyone can be negative. Anyone can throw up his arms and say the church has no business dabbling in this or that issue. Anyone can condemn others who have tried to give answers to these issues. But it takes considerable grace, wisdom, charity, and honesty to offer solutions that will give positive guidance to the members of the discussion group who want to face the issues realistically.

Most issues do not have cut-and-dried solutions. It may take considerable thought and discussion to arrive at adequate answers. You will find that on some of the issues the only suitable solution is a consensus of opinion. On others, your group will come up with dynamic answers and actions. In each case, the authors sincerely hope that the end result will produce Christian solutions that apply to the various issues as they present themselves in local communities and in the nation. As group members discuss these issues, and think through toward positive answers, they will be better equipped to face the world where these issues are constantly raised.

Contents

Should Christians Support the "Women's Revolution"? 1

THE ROLE OF WOMEN IN SOCIETY is becoming an increasingly explosive issue. The emancipated woman is asserting her liberty with militancy and aggressiveness. The fight for suffrage in the early 1900s may have been only a mild revolution compared to what may be in store. Women are organizing once again to assert more of their "basic rights." They intend to live as "free women" without the strictures of masculine society to keep them tied down to demeaning domesticity.

Modern suffragettes have been called "new feminists," "women liberators," and "women revolutionaries." They use various and fancy titles to describe themselves: WITCH (Women's International Terrorist Conspiracy from Hell), WRAP (Women's Radical Action Project), and WOLF (Women's Liberation Front). These are some of their more flamboyant titles. A group called NOW (National Organization for Women), with over 3,000 members, tries to transform beliefs into action by doing such things as establishing day-care centers for working mothers. No matter what they call themselves, women are becoming aroused, vocal, and determined to see that they get the respect, equality and opportunities they deserve.

The outcry of the new feminists is that they are an oppressed minority, excluded from positions of power, exploited by male dominance (male chauvinism)

11

sexually, economically, and in almost every other way. The new feminists list statistics to prove their charges: 51 percent of Americans are female, yet only one percent of American engineers are women, only 3 percent are lawyers, only 7 percent are doctors. On top of these inequities, women get paid less for the same jobs. While median wages and salaries for men were $4,713 in 1957, for women they were $3,008. In 1968, the average income for men rose to $7,800 — (65 percent), but the average income for women went up to only $4,550 — (51 percent). This was a wider gap than in 1957!

Women don't hold enough positions of power and influence, according to the new feminists. They have held only 50 seats in state legislatures in the past ten years. In 1968, only one woman was in the United States Senate. There were only ten congresswomen, compared with 17 in 1960. Even feminine influence in education has dwindled through the years. Faculty positions held in colleges have been reduced from more than one-third to less than one-fourth in the last 70 years.

Women militants look at these inequities and believe something should be done. Some of their actions are merely symbolic (such as picketing the Miss America Pageant, hurling padded bras, false eyelashes, and *Playboy* magazines into "freedom" trash cans) to draw attention, and perhaps laughs, to their cause. They have learned that the shock value, such as used by civil rights groups, is a good way to get a hearing.

But the new feminists don't simply want publicity or minor reforms. As one writer in *McCall's* put it: "They have much more on their minds than one particular reform, such as the 1920 fight to win the vote. What many of them want today is nothing short of changing the world, restructuring society, turning upside down all the accepted attitudes that have been deeply ingrained in our collective consciousness since forever — attitudes about the role of the man (the big, strong, attractive one, who cuts down trees for the fire, builds houses, protects the family, goes to work, has most of the muscles and brains, and makes most of the money) and the role of the woman (the weak and sexy one, who has the babies, cooks the casseroles, cleans, sews, washes, is motherly, brotherly, a nurse, lover, is always available and compliant).

"The new feminists reject the idea that millions of women could possibly be happy just raising babies, cooking, and caring for their husbands and the house. They prefer to think of these housewives as having been brainwashed into accepting the role of the domestic slave and concubine, a sex object used for pleasure and breeding purposes, as well. They further reject the idea, which they think is prevalent, that women in business and the professions are naturally better suited to being secretaries, nurses, librarians, lab technicians, draftswomen, assistants to men than to being executive trainees, doctors, lawyers, scientists, editors, architects, or directors of their own programs and departments. This, say the feminists, is an obsolete and degrading conception of the nature of women."[1]

While much of what some of the new feminists want may infuriate most men, perhaps the women are making some gains by focusing attention on certain inequities and misunderstandings. *Time* says: "They have, for example, exposed the myth that a woman's income is mostly a supplement: a third of all women of marriageable age are not married; two-thirds of working women, whether married or not, work because they need the money. Thirty-six percent of the nation's families get their primary income from women. Considered in this light, what seems a monotonous litany of the need for better wage scales and good day-care centers assumes more urgency (2,700,-

000 children need day-care centers; there are places for 530,000).

"Men, for reasons entirely of their own, may soon agree to some of the changes the feminists propose, and indeed over 100 males are members of NOW. New studies show that many men actually want women to combine careers and families, that most women also want both careers and families, but that they *think* the men want them to stay home. (Just publicizing the studies ought to help eliminate this misunderstanding.) Moreover, what was once a natural and universally admired goal — to have a large family — may, with the threat of overpopulation, be seen as mere self-indulgence. Population experts are already proposing tax changes and legal restrictions to keep families small. As part of the same program, they suggest that women be given education and job opportunities equal to those accorded men."[2]

Some women militants refer to the bondage that women have endured as a hangover from biblical tradition and morals. They have cited the apostle Paul's apparent negative attitude toward marriage (I Cor. 7:8), his call to wifely obedience and submission (Eph. 5:22; Col. 3:18), and his statement that women should play a silent and submissive role in the church (I Cor. 14:34; I Tim. 2:11, 12) as examples of Paul's prejudice. Perhaps they are using the Bible as a kind of whipping post. While it is true the apostle reflects the traditions of his time, it is not quite fair to say that the Bible has fostered the subjugation of women as slaves or as things.

On the contrary, it has been shown by biblical scholars that the teachings of Christianity differ profoundly from those of the cultures of the time. Jesus showed a deep concern and appreciation for women (cf. John 4; John 8:2-11; John 20:11-18). A careful study of the New Testament clearly shows a sharp contrast between the biblical attitude toward women and that which prevailed in the heathen cultures of the day.

Nancy Goodwin has given a Christian perspective to women's newly found freedom. Mrs. Goodwin, writing in *Eternity* before the current storm, presented some valuable insights she gleaned from Betty Friedan's book, *The Feminine Mystique* (Betty Friedan founded NOW in 1966). Mrs. Goodwin says:

"I found Mrs. Friedan's remarks on housework were most applicable to Christian wives. Our traditional (more than scriptural) image embodies the feminine mystique, with slightly less glamorous sex appeal, and slightly more church activity. Her image is the happy, fulfilled, spiritual homemaker. She tacks verses and prayers around and says them on the run. Why is she on the run? She spends most of her time having babies, raising them and providing her husband with the things a Christian man can seemingly wallow in without guilt — comfort, food, and sex.

"Today's Christian woman would be better off if she would follow the example of the woman in Proverbs 31 — use her free time, not expanding her housework, but developing an ability for which she will be paid; then studying the conditions of the poor and using her earnings to relieve their suffering. She could study methods for starting neighborhood Bible studies and put her free energies into that. She should be developing friendships with non-Christians and witnessing to them — not gossiping over the back fence.

"Christian wives are too busy pampering their husbands and children and by this process all are weakened rather than strengthened. Father must eat the food that Mother has worked so hard over all day. He must rest in his retreat. What is a better formula for flabbiness and overweight? Mother must not be distracted from her homemaking. What is a better formula for losing contact with the suspicious outside world, thus making effective communication with intelligent non-Christians extremely difficult for her?"[3]

It is no doubt true that not all women accept or even desire to have their role drastically changed. Many women still prefer the old-fashioned femininity which centers in family relationships and traditional moral values. The radicals who wish to do away with marriage as we know it in the Western World, who mistrust all men, and who could care less about children and the propagation of the race are doubtless a minority. Neither is there unanimity in thought among the militant women. Their ambivalence stretches from sex as a distasteful game that only pleases men to free love and trial marriage as valid options. The task for the Christian woman is to find the right balance of values in the light of biblical teaching and their own intelligence. The biblical picture of man's relation to woman and woman's relation to man is our best hope.

WHAT DOES THE BIBLE SAY?

"So God created man in his own image, in the image of God created he him; male and female created he them" (Gen. 1:27).

"But I would have you know, that the head of every man is Christ; and the head of the woman is the man; and the head of Christ is God. For a man indeed ought not to cover his head, forasmuch as he is the image and glory of God; but the woman is the glory of the man. For the man is not of the woman; but the woman of the man. Neither was the man created for the woman; but the woman for the man. Nevertheless neither is the man without the woman, neither the woman without the man, in the Lord. For as the woman is of the man, even so is the man also by the woman; but all things of God" (I Cor. 11:3, 7-9, 11-12).

"In like manner also, that women adorn themselves in modest apparel, with shamefacedness
and sobriety, not with braided hair, or gold, or
pearls, or costly array; But (which becometh
women professing godliness) with good works.
Let the woman learn in silence with all subjection. But I suffer not a woman to teach, nor to
usurp authority over the man, but to be in silence.
For Adam was first formed, then Eve. And
Adam was not deceived, but the woman being
deceived was in the transgression" (I Tim. 2:9-
14).

" . . . There is neither male nor female: for ye
are all one in Christ Jesus" (Gal. 3:28).

"Submitting yourselves one to another in the fear
of God. Wives, submit yourselves unto your own
husbands, as unto the Lord. For the husband is
the head of the wife, even as Christ is the head
of the church: and he is the savior of the body.
Therefore as the church is subject unto Christ, so
let the wives be to their own husbands in every
thing. Husbands, love your wives, even as Christ
also loved the church, and gave himself for it.
So ought men to love their wives as their own
bodies. He that loveth his wife loveth himself.
Nevertheless, let every one of you in particular
so love his wife even as himself; and the wife
see that she reverence her husband" (Eph. 5:21-
25, 28, 33).

"Likewise, ye wives, be in subjection to your
own husbands; that, if any obey not the word,
they also may without the word be won by the
conversation [behavior] of the wives; While they
behold your chaste conversation coupled with
fear. Whose adorning, let it not be that outward

adorning of plaiting [braiding] the hair, and of wearing of gold, or of putting on of apparel; But let it be the hidden man of the heart in that which is not corruptible, even the ornament of a meek and quiet spirit, which is in the sight of God of great price. For after this manner in the old time the holy women also, who trusted in God, adorned themselves, being in subjection unto their own husbands. Likewise, ye husbands dwell with them according to knowledge, giving honor unto the wife, as unto the weaker vessel, and as being heirs together of the grace of life; that your prayers be not hindered" (I Pet. 3:1-5, 7). (Also see Proverbs 31:10-31.)

WHAT DO YOU SAY?

1. What is the biblical view of women? Are women inferior to men? Does the creation story imply that man is in some sense higher or better than woman?

2. What biblical evidence shows that women have an equality with men? In what sense are they equal? In what sense are they not?

3. The Bible speaks of woman as being the "weaker vessel." How is this so? In what ways are women stronger than men?

4. How does the physical structure and stature of man (body build and strength, etc.) as compared to woman (smaller body, smaller muscles, etc.) relate to the limitation of a woman's role in society? Is body build a valid basis for discrimination for certain occupations?

5. What is the significance of the new movements toward freeing women from domestic chores, child rearing, etc.? Does it indicate a moving away from biblical values?

6. What is the meaning of the biblical command for wives to "obey" and be "in subjection" to their husbands? Why is the emphasis on the husband to "love" his wife? Should not the husband and the wife both "love and obey"?

7. Is there any biblical reason why a woman cannot have a career and also care for her family? What are the drawbacks of having both a career and a family to maintain?

8. Should Christian mothers with children at home avoid involvement in careers? Is it true that "a woman's place is in the home"?

9. How can husbands make their wives feel they are not "discriminated" against because they are women? What is the meaning of I Peter 3:7?

10. Are women really being discriminated against today, or is all the current fuss just the spirit of the times and a good cure for boredom?

11. What is the husband's responsibility toward his family in relationship to the place of the wife in the home? Is the "breadwinner" role a valid one? Why or why not?

12. How has the emancipated woman benefited society? Is it really a sociological advance or simply an economic necessity in our technological society?

Notes

1. Leslie Aldrige Westoff, "Is a Women's Revolution Really Possible? Yes," *McCall's*, October 1969. Used by permission.

2. "The New Feminists: Revolt Against Sexism," *Time*, November 21, 1969. Used by permission.

3. Nancy Goodwin, "Feminine Mistake," *Eternity*, September 1964. Used by permission.

Where Is Space Exploration Taking Us? 2

THE ORBITING OF RUSSIA'S SPUTNIK I launched mankind into a new era. Man can no longer consider himself simply a creature of the earth. He is now a creature of the universe.

During the 1970s, there will be many more space spectaculars. Plans include spacecraft capable of staying aloft as long as 56 days with 12 men aboard; landing on Mars; penetration of Venus' atmosphere by manned craft; regular excursions to the moon. Some envision what has been called the "Grand Tour" — a spacecraft flying past Jupiter, Saturn, Uranus, and Neptune.

Voyages to other worlds are no longer the fantasies of science fiction writers. They are scientific possibilities in our lifetime.

Dr. Thomas O. Paine, administrator of the National Aeronautics and Space Administration states, "The space program has brought man to the threshold of a new era — an era in which man will expand his domain from the tiny 8,000-mile-diameter earth on which he was born outward into the 8-billion-mile-diameter solar system, and beyond that perhaps some day to the stars."

Dr. Paine goes on to say, "Modern space technology is opening a new frontier for man of infinite extent, and endless frontier. Our pioneering astronauts have blazed a trail for all future generations of men who want to set forth to conquer new worlds. I think history will record this as the greatest contribution of our generation. Through man's brain, energy, and resources, life can — and life will — extend itself throughout the solar system."[1]

Beyond the sudden awareness of our ability to conquer space, an ability many Christians previously believed would never be allowed by God, can only be the limits of man's dreams. Now that Christians have survived the initial shock of man's space exploits, and have joined in the thrills created by our scientific achievements some new problems arise. What if space adventurers discover some form of life on other planets? Such a find could have a tremendous impact on much of man's thinking, and would perhaps force Christians to rethink such things as their views of God and the possibilities of salvation for "people" on other planets.

Nobel Prize winning Dr. Harold Clayton Urey, interviewed for *Forbes Magazine* by Mary Harrington Hall, said, "If man doesn't explore, then he doesn't exist. That's what he's for. We are compelled by our intellect to do these things, and engineering is a plastic realization of what we think about. This is the nature of man himself. . . . It is no more possible for man *not* to go to the moon than for Picasso *not* to paint."

When Mary Hall asked, "What has science done for religion?" Urey answered: "I would have been burned at the stake in 1600 for going one step further than Copernicus. But I think what we've done in science during these years is to give men a much bigger view of the universe. And — if there is a God — He is a much greater God than anyone ever imagined before. I think the space program has dramatized facts of this kind. The architecture of the universe is far more wondrous than man could have believed in centuries past. . . . Science is spoiling people's simple

21

trust in a religion that gives a noble purpose for existing, no matter how disappointing things are. This is a practical thing religion does for people, and science supplies nothing to substitute for it."[2]

Dr. Wernher von Braun, who first developed rockets in Germany for Hitler during World War II, and who is presently director of the National Aeronautics and Space Administration's George C. Marshall Space Flight Center, Huntsville, Ala., has been led to a fuller understanding of the Creator through his probes into space science. He believes that God will open up even greater knowledge of the universe. He says he finds it as difficult to understand "a scientist who does not acknowledge the presence of a superior rationality behind the existence of the universe as it is to comprehend a theologian who would deny the advances of science. There is certainly no scientific reason why God cannot retain the same position in our modern world that He held before we began probing His creation with telescope and cyclotron."

He continues, "God has built man with curiosity. God expects man to use this gift. Now we have the tools available to explore space and I believe if it were not the Creator's intent for us to explore celestial bodies, He would not have permitted us to have acquired the tools.

"Something else is apparent. God has not placed any visible obstacles in our way. I believe we have His permission and His blessing. . . ; by setting up observation stations in outer space, we will have a platform to learn far more about the universe. Through a closer look at creation, we ought to gain a better knowledge of the Creator, and a greater sense of man's responsibility to God will come into focus."[3]

Some Christians have fears about finding life on other planets. Because their carefully constructed theological system makes man God's most important creature, and limits redemption to a narrow theological framework, they have reservations about intelligent life on other planets. They also wonder if God would redeem other planet "people" through a way other than the biblical revelation of redemption.

Alphred D. O'Hare, chief of Launch Vehicle Operations Management Office, Cape Kennedy, says, "Is there life on other celestial bodies, either planet-like life or other bodies with immortal souls? I would not be shocked to find that such life did exist nor would I be shocked to find that it did not. . . . One point is very clear to me: just because the law of probabilities indicates that life must in fact exist because of the magnitude of the numbers of bodies in the heavens does not make it so. If extraterrestrial life exists, it is because God has willed it to be so. God is not constrained to probability or limited by sophisticated computer prognostications."[4]

A somewhat contrary view is presented in the same discussion by Dr. John C. Whitcomb, Jr., director of postgraduate studies, Grace Theological Seminary, Winona Lake, Ind. He says, "It has become my increasing conviction that intelligent life does *not* exist on other planets. In the first place, astronomers have failed to demonstrate that any other planet exists in the universe that possesses the right conditions for life. Even more important, a century of post-Darwinian research has only succeeded in showing that spontaneous generation and macroevolution are incompatible with the known laws of nature throughout the universe. Therefore, if intelligent life exists elsewhere, God would have to have created it and its environment supernaturally. But in His special revelation in Scripture, God very strongly implies that the planet Earth is unique in the universe as a home for intelligent beings with physical bodies. When the Creator of the universe became a permanent member of the human race through the incarnation (John 1:14) and promised that He would return to this planet to establish His kingdom (Acts 1:11), He demonstrated His concern for mankind is not a passing one or a temporary one."[5]

Where is space exploration taking us? Perhaps to some critical reassessment of our present theological views about the nature and scope of God's redemption. Perhaps to some different views about ourselves and our ability to cope with extraterrestrial life. Whatever space research may open up to us as Christians, we cannot be satisfied with closed theological systems. We must also do some exploring into our own theology and into the Word of God so that we will be prepared with a "theology for the space age" for a future that will most likely reveal wonders of the universe beyond our comprehension.

WHAT DOES THE BIBLE SAY?

"Thus saith the Lord . . . I have made the earth, and created man upon it: I, even my hands, have stretched out the heavens, and all their host have I commanded. I have raised him up in righteousness, and I will direct all his ways . . ." (Isa. 45: 11-13).

"And I gave my heart to seek and search out by wisdom concerning all things that are done under heaven: this sore travail hath God given to to the sons of men to be exercised therewith" (Eccl. 1:13).

"The heavens declare the glory of God; and the firmament showeth his handywork. Day unto day uttereth speech, and night unto night showeth knowledge" (Ps. 19:1, 2).

"Looking for and hasting unto the coming of the day of God, wherein the heavens being on fire shall be dissolved, and the elements shall melt with fervent heat? Nevertheless we, according to his promise, look for new heavens and a new earth, wherein dwelleth righteousness" (II Pet. 3:12, 13).

"And I will show wonders in heaven above, and signs in the earth beneath; blood, and fire, and vapor of smoke: The sun shall be turned into darkness, and the moon into blood, before that great and notable day of the Lord come: And it shall come to pass, that whosoever shall call on the name of the Lord shall be saved" (Acts 2: 19-21).

"For the invisible things of him from the creation of the world are clearly seen, being understood by the things that are made, even his eternal power and Godhead . . ." (Rom. 1:20).

"He stretcheth out the north over the empty place, and hangeth the earth upon nothing. The pillars of heaven tremble, and are astonished at his reproof. By his Spirit he hath garnished the heavens; his hand hath formed the crooked serpent" (Job 26:7, 11, 13).

"By the word of the Lord were the heavens made; and all the host of them by the breath of his mouth. Let all the earth fear the Lord: let all the inhabitants of the world stand in awe of him. For he spake, and it was done; he commanded, and it stood fast" (Ps. 33:6, 8, 9).

WHAT DO YOU SAY?

1. How can space exploration affect our concept of God? Does it enhance our concept of God's transcendence or immanence? Will it make us less dependent on Him or more so?

2. What theological significance — as far as man's nature is concerned — can we apply to current space explorations?

3. Does Scripture limit the sphere of space exploration? If so, in what ways?

4. How would you explain the existence of intelligent life, if any, on other planets in the light of biblical knowledge? Would the Bible be proven false or incomplete?

5. Why is it getting more difficult to believe in the evolutionary theory of the development of the universe? Would life on other planets add to or take away from the credibility of this theory? How?

6. In the light of the magnitude of problems within our society, should Christians attempt to slow down the space race in order to spend more money to cure society's ills? What would you suggest?

7. How have space probes forced Christians to change their previously held views? Are these new attitudes beneficial or detrimental to a belief in the gospel? Explain.

8. Do you think that interplanetary exploration will add anything to a Christian's view of God? the world? himself? Christ?

9. What justifies risking men's lives and spending vast amounts of money to obtain new knowledge of the moon, earth, planets, sun or stars? What are the ethical implications of this?

10. Are the side benefits of the space program which improve the quality of our life on the earth good enough reasons to maintain research at the present level?

11. If there were intelligent creatures on other planets, would Christians have a responsibility to take the gospel to them? Why or why not?

Notes

1. Thomas O. Paine, quoted by Ronald Kotulak, "After the Moon, What?" *Chicago Tribune Magazine,* November 9, 1969. Reprinted by permission, Copyright © 1969 World Rights Reserved. Chicago Tribune Company.

2. Harold Clayton Urey, "As I See It," *Forbes Magazine,* July 15, 1969. Used by permission.

3. Wernher von Braun, quoted by Adon Taft, "Why Has God Allowed Us into Space?" *Christian Life,* July 1969. Used by permission of Christian Life Publications, Inc., Gundersen Drive and Schmale Road, Wheaton, Illinois 60187.

4. Alphred D. O'Hare, in a panel discussion, "The Christian Stake in Space," reprinted from *Moody Monthly,* July-August, 1969. Used by permission. Copyright 1969, Moody Bible Institute of Chicago.

5. John C. Whitcomb, Jr., *Ibid.*

Interracial Marriage – Good or Bad? 3

THE IDEA OF INTERRACIAL MARRIAGE TROUBLES many people, including Christians. The reasons behind these hang-ups are complex and rooted deep in our history and culture. Prejudice dominates much thinking on the subject, rather than anthropological, sociological or even biblical considerations. Both blacks and whites have prejudiced attitudes toward the issue of interracial marriage. It is extreme racial pride that feels it is only the black person who really wants to marry a white, or vice versa.

The question of interracial marriage is considered crucial by some because prevalent attitudes toward it are a yardstick to measure the progress of integration. Andrew Billingsley points out in his book, *Black Families in White America*, that "marriage among peoples of different cultural backgrounds is considered, by many students of assimilation, to be the ultimate test of the process of integration, as well as of whether a caste system exists, separating two peoples into superior and inferior beings. In these respects, then, the question of interracial marriage is more than a matter of personal choice; it is an index of the view and place of different peoples in the national life."[1]

The problem of interracial marriage is particularly great in the United States because of our long history of racial problems and misunderstandings. Interracial marriage has been forbidden by laws from the times of slavery to modern times. It was not until 1967 that the United States Supreme Court ruled against all such laws.

Even though there has been an increase in the number of interracial marriages in the United States, there has not been any significant change of attitudes among Americans. In a 1968 Gallup poll among 15,-000 people in 13 countries, the United States showed 72 percent (the highest of all countries polled) disapproval of marriages between whites and nonwhites. Only 20 percent approved, while 8 percent had no opinion.

Even though public attitudes are slowly changing, Christians have generally been opposed to interracial dating and marriage. Some hold very extreme views and maintain that their position is solidly based on the Bible. Perhaps a representative of one of the more extreme views comes from Evangelist J. Harold Smith, a radio preacher in Dallas, Texas. Here are some excerpts from one of his sermons: " . . . both history and the Bible reveal that any nation or people practicing intermarriage of the races soon lose both their national and racial prestige. . . . God Almighty never has, and never will, put His approval upon the marriage of different colors. My friends, as sure as that takes place, whether it is in Rome, whether it is in Greece, whether it is among the white and the black, or the white and the yellow, or the yellow and the black, *that race loses its identity.* Neighbors, God Almighty, down through these years, has preserved the races. . . . Any individual or organization in America, or any other nation, that teaches, preaches, or propagates intermarriages of the *races* is of the *devil! No nation can remain strong unless her people remain racially pure! This is according to God's decree!*"[2]

Mr. Smith uses several Scripture passages commonly cited to support the separation of the races

(Acts 17:26; Gen. 9:24-27; Gen. 10:32; Deut. 7:1-3; Josh. 23:12, 13; Ezra 9:12; Deut. 22:9-11).

A revealing contrast, showing the wide divergence among Christians on this issue, comes in the statements of Dr. Bob Jones, Jr. and Dr. John Warwick Montgomery.

Dr. Jones says, "Fallen man has been trying to break down God's boundaries and build One World ever since the Tower of Babel. Man is attempting to achieve without the reign of Jesus Christ what God intends shall come only to the Glory of His Son. The cry today is, 'One World, One Race, One Church,' but it will be a corrupt and evil world, a mongrel race, and the church of Antichrist. Intermarriage of the races is a breakdown of the lines of separation which God has set up and, therefore, is rebellion against God."[3]

Dr. Montgomery says, "Racial integration is thoroughly Christian, for God created all men and Christ died for all men. The consequence is that 'there is neither Jew nor Greek: ye are all one in Christ Jesus' (Gal. 3:28). One of the greatest blots on the history of American churches is their toleration of the prejudicial treatment of minority races. No legitimate effort should be spared to help Negroes and other minorities to achieve full civil and social rights — and this requires direct opposition to unjust and immoral legislation (which, as a matter of fact, is not genuine legislation at all when it stands in opposition to God's eternal law!). 'But, Dr. Montgomery, would you want *your* daughter to marry one of them?' In a word, Yes! Better that my daughter should marry a believing Negro than a bigoted White who has forgotten the love of Christ and 'passed by on the other side!' "[4]

Many of the reasons given for opposing marriage between people of different races or colors are based on the sociological and pyschological effects that are purported to make such marriages undesirable. Opponents of intermarriage often question the motives of people who decide to marry a person of another race. Love is often denied as the real reason.

Many people are bound by common racial stereotypes rooted in prejudice and fear. One such stereotype is that of sexuality: "A common belief runs that the white girl who marries a Negro is morally depraved and certainly sexually abnormal, for no *normal* white woman could possibly enjoy the average Negro's savage sexual potency. As for the white man who marries a Negro woman, he will soon 'tire of her extraordinary sensuality and return to the safer, saner sex practices' of his own kind. Such assertions, made by the majority race with all the blatant insistence of an uneasy conscience, have conditioned the Negro sufficiently to prevent his speaking out in favor of intermarriage. But no one has bothered to validate the declarations of sexual incompatibility between the races with scientific investigations. . . . That such incompatibility exists between normal individuals of the two races is an emotion-based assumption which finds sanction and support in statutes prohibiting intermarriage. Such statutes seem to me to be the most fundamental expression of the human inequality to which the Negro is subjected. They strike at the deepest roots of personal dignity and self-respect."[5] Even though such statutes may no longer exist, attitudes that persist even among Christians perpetuate an undeserved indignity upon black people.

Other reasons behind intermarriage, according to some, are rebellion against parents and society, attraction to opposites, the attractiveness of something that is considered taboo. A white woman may associate with a black man because of some depraved concept of herself as a woman and the Negro as a man. A black man may look upon a white woman as a socially identifiable female ideal with an extremely

31

exciting sexuality. She becomes a target for a hatred that goes further than the man-woman relationship. Or perhaps attraction to a person of another race is caused by a hatred of oneself. Or is it just an extreme way for people to prove to themselves and to society that they are *not* racist?

These and other stereotypes may or may not have validity in each particular case. No one can fully judge the individual reasons and the complex factors that go into personal relationships between people, regardless of race. Perhaps society should not be asking what motivates people of different races to intermarry; rather they should be asking why society seeks to know. Can we honestly treat people as human beings and continue asking such questions? Aren't such questions motivated by prejudices and traces of racism deeply rooted in our hearts?

People do not generally accept interracial couples. Some carry their hostilities and resentments to the point of accusing the interracially married couples of committing some wrong personally against society. This hostility of prejudiced people is itself an argument used against intermarriage. People ask, "What will happen to your children?" "What will your friends think?" "What will your parents say?" "What about your parents' friends?" "What about your children's children?" Certainly all such questions are not valid or reasonable, nevertheless they are continually asked. Perhaps we should not put so much weight on them. These are society's questions, not those of the two people who happen to love one another.

Christian Life, in an article on "Interracial Marriage," by Hilda Bryant, considers some of these objections by citing actual cases of intermarriage. Mrs. Bryant refers to a survey made by the Seattle Urban League in 1966. It was taken from a random sampling of 75 couples out of 250 known interracial couples.

"The study concluded that interracial couples in Seattle have a high educational background and many are engaged in professional work or are on the management level. That such couples and their children will be rebuffed by both races, by their neighbors and by their relatives did not hold up across the board. Their children, the survey indicated, are carrying no special burden. Most said that the arrival of children brought understanding and healed breaches.

"However, the answers on the questionnaires confirmed the contention that Negro-white couples encounter considerably more discrimination than other interracially married couples, particularly in housing and employment. This is not because of their marriage but because of discrimination against the Negro partner. Negro-white marriages proved to be traumatic to relatives, in some cases cutting the couple off from their families.

"Of the Negro-white couples responding to the survey, 68.4 percent attended college; about one-third went to graduate school. About one-fourth of the Negro-white children identified with both races. Another fourth seems oblivious of the need. Generally in this country if a child is half black he is considered a Negro. Whether or not Negro-white marriages are a handicap in employment depends a great deal on the field. . . . Of the Negro-white couples, 42.6 percent were employed professionals or on the management level. Only 14 percent of the Negro-white couples surveyed said their marriage was a handicap in getting a job."[6]

Mrs. Bryant asks a significant question concerning whether a Christian Caucasian can marry a Christian Negro and expect a successful marriage by scriptural standards. One of the couples interviewed (Marna and Ed Matthews), highly dedicated and intelligent Christians, found little discrimination that mattered to

33

them. Ed summed up his view this way, "I see as my purpose letting people know that Christ is the most important Person to me and that He feels that I am important to Him no matter of what race I am. Our marriage is based on the teachings of Christ, and I think this is a foundation strong enough. My education helps — it helps to be able to go to work every day, to have a definite income and not worry about getting fired. I think there would be more hang-ups with a Catholic-Protestant marriage than with an interracial one."[7]

As a result of Mrs. Bryant's case studies she concluded: "There are discernible trends that cannot be ignored. Most significantly, the question, 'Can a Christian interracial marriage be successful by scriptural standards?' must be answered 'Yes.'

"A second inevitable question, 'Will such a couple suffer discrimination?' must also be answered, 'Yes.' Overt expressions of prejudice particularly can be expected in their search for acceptable housing, occasionally in employment and in almost every case there will be problems of acceptance by one or the other immediate families.

"It seems apparent, too, that mixed-race children usually are not mistreated. With racial tolerance rapidly increasing throughout the nation, hostility aimed at interracial children rapidly may become a thing of the past."[8]

WHAT DOES THE BIBLE SAY?

"And I will make thee swear by the Lord, the God of heaven, and the God of the earth, that thou shalt not take a wife unto my son of the daughters of the Canaanites, among whom I dwell" (Gen. 24:3).

"And Isaac called Jacob, and blessed him, and charged him, and said unto him, Thou shalt not take a wife of the daughters of Canaan" (Gen. 28:1).

"And if a stranger sojourn with thee in your land, ye shall not vex him. But the stranger who dwelleth with you shall be unto you as one born among you, and thou shalt love him as thyself . . ." (Lev. 19:33, 34).

"When the Most High divided to the nations their inheritance, when he separated the sons of Adam he set the bounds of the people according to the number of the children of Israel" (Deut. 32:8).

" . . .The land, unto which ye go to possess it, is an unclean land with the filthiness of the people of the lands, with their abomination, which have filled it from one end to another with their uncleanness. Now therefore give not your daughters unto their sons, neither take their daughters unto your sons, nor seek their peace or their wealth for ever; that ye may be strong, and eat the good of the land, and leave it for an inheritance to your children for ever" (Ezra 9:11, 12).

"Have we not all one father? hath not one God created us? why do we deal treacherously every man against his brother, by profaning the covenant of our fathers?" (Mal. 2:10).

" . . . Have ye not read, that he who made them at the beginning made them male and female, And said, For this cause shall a man leave father and mother, and shall cleave to his wife: and they twain shall be one flesh? Wherefore they are no more twain, but one flesh. What therefore God hath joined together, let not man put asunder" (Matt. 19:4-6).

"Then Peter opened his mouth, and said, Of a truth I perceive that God is no respecter of persons: But in every nation he that feareth him, and worketh righteousness, is accepted with him" (Acts 10:34, 35).

"And hath made of one blood all nations of men for to dwell on all the face of the earth, and hath determined the times before appointed, and the bounds of their habitation" (Acts 17:26).

"There is neither Jew nor Greek, there is neither bond nor free, there is neither male nor female: for ye are all one in Christ Jesus" (Gal. 3:28).

"My brethren, have not the faith of our Lord Jesus Christ, the Lord of glory, with respect of persons. . . . But if ye have respect of persons, ye commit sin" (James 2:1, 9a).

WHAT DO YOU SAY?

1. Are there any biological or anthropological reasons to prohibit intermarriage of different races? Is there such a thing as a "pure" race?

2. In view of the biblical teaching of the unity of the human race, is there any ground for separating the races by prohibiting intermarriage?

3. How do you explain Moses' marriage to an Ethiopian (Cushite) in Numbers 12:1? Was God's anger and judgment on Miriam (v. 9, 10) evidence of God's approval on Moses?

4. Are the biblical injunctions against marrying non-Israelites valid references to use against interracial marriage? Do they have primary reference to purity of race or purity of faith?

5. Is the practice of applying Scripture against interracial marriage a form of racism? Does Scripture condone racism in any form?

6. Is the argument that interracial marriage is in-

advisable because people will show hostility to both parents and children a valid one?

7. Such Scripture passages as Gen. 24:3, 4, Gen. 28:1, Ezra 9:12, and Gen. 9:25-27, are said by some to prove that God is against "mongrelizing" the races. Is such interpretation a correct or distorted use of Scripture?

8. Why do people question the motives of people of different races who want to marry? Is such questioning right? Should not all people who want to marry be subjected to the same type of questioning and doubting?

9. If two Christians of different races love each other and are "one in Christ," what biblical or other reason would make such a marriage wrong? Is such discrimination right?

10. How can Christians show understanding toward interracially married people? Could an interracially married couple join your church? If not, why not?

11. Why is the question of interracial marriage so vital to the progress of integration? Can there be true integration without intermarriage?

12. Is racism expressed in violent denunciations of integration and intermarriage a form of evil pride condemned by the Bible?

Notes

1. Andrew Billingsley, *Black Families in White America*, © 1968, p. 65. Used by permission of Prentice-Hall, Inc.

2. J. Harold Smith, "God's Plan for the Races, America's Number One Problem, Segregation," Radio Bible Hour, Dallas, Texas.

3. Robert Campbell, ed., *Spectrum of Protestant Beliefs*, p. 68. Used by permission of The Bruce Publishing Company.

4. *Ibid.*, p. 69.

5. Saunders Redding, *On Being Negro in America*, p. 113. Copyright © 1951. Reprinted by permission of the publisher, The Bobbs-Merrill Company, Inc.

6. Hilda Bryant, "Interracial Marriage," *Christian Life*, January 1969. Used by permission of Christian Life Publications, Inc. Gundersen Drive and Schmale Road, Wheaton, Illinois 60187.

7. *Ibid.*

8. *Ibid.*

Does the "Medium" Have a Message? 4

THE STARTLING INCREASE OF INTEREST in psychic phenomena and the spirit world has become a growing concern for Christians. The Christian's interest in spiritism stems from the prohibitions given in the Bible against consulting mediums and wizards, and from the standpoint of the reality of the spiritual world. While Christians cannot condone the practice of consulting spirits, they are interested in such supernatural phenomena as it relates to the questions and implications of the "other world" and life after death — doctrines categorically denied by modern scientific man.

Scientific methodology based on verifying facts and technology built on observable data have not dampened human interest in the "other side." Perhaps the rise of interest in supernatural and psychic phenomena is a reaction to the calculated, impersonal, and automated world of science. In fact, the widespread practice of consulting mediums and contacting spirits has come under scientific investigation. The Institute of Parapsychology in Durham, North Carolina, has been studying such things as predicting the future and extrasensory perception (ESP). In over 40 years of intense research, they have shown that some kind of perception does exist beyond the normal senses. Tests have been made with playing cards, where psychics were able to predict, before they were shuffled, the resulting sequence of a deck of cards and to name the hidden sides of cards from miles away, with chance being an unlikely possibility.

Some psychics have been consulted in crime investigation cases and have come up with revealing, if not convincing, observations. Jeanne Dixon, the famous forecaster, predicted the assassination of President Kennedy, the fall of Malenkov in 1955, and the orbiting of Sputnik in 1957. Psychics have been mistaken, of course. Perhaps a large majority of mediums and seers are nothing more than clever people with a keen sensitivity to human nature and gullibility.

Enough evidence seems to have been amassed to safely say that spiritual phenomena, ESP and the "gift of prophecy" is a world of reality, whether demonic or not. Such evidence makes it important that these phenomena be confronted and evaluated by Christians. Christian revelation demands that such phenomena be taken seriously. An honest evaluation will help Christians avoid being taken in by modern interpretations of the supernatural.

Some modern-day disciples of the spirit world claim that psychic experiments are of value to Christians. Arthur Ford, a well-known clergyman and psychic, and founder of Spiritual Frontiers Fellowship, who had a TV séance with Rev. James Pike a few years ago said, "Psychic experiment has brought to thousands of Christians not fear but its opposite — great strength, hope and courage. Everybody has psychic ability, be it ever so little, waiting to be developed. The psychic gift is the breath of God in each individual. In I Corinthians 12, Paul lists healing, prophecy and the ability to distinguish between spirits, all 'inspired by one and the same spirit.' If your motive is God-centered, you are free to explore anything in the universe without fear. The new parapsychology, very close to the earliest insights of Christianity, is not a study of isolated phenomena but of the whole nature of man. People survive death whether

40

they are good or bad, Christian or not — this is the factual basis of Christianity. After 'death' you wake up the same person you were when you went to sleep. This is not a setting aside of natural law but the realization of a divine potential."[1]

Merrill F. Unger, Old Testament scholar and author of *Biblical Demonology,* takes a different view. He says, "The distinguishing feature of modern spiritism, frequently misnamed 'spiritualism,' is its purported intercourse with the spirits of the dead. In this, it is identical with ancient necromancy. Although much that passes for present-day spiritistic manifestation is pure chicanery, nevertheless, that real communications from the spirit-world are at times received, cannot for one moment be doubted, if both scriptural and non-scriptural evidence is to be given credence.

"Facts are not lacking to indicate that modern spiritism is nothing more nor less than ancient sorcery revived, with particular emphasis on communication with the supposed spirits of the dead, which are really deceiving, impersonating demons, so that the phenomenon is basically demonism. Its modern claim of being a 'new dispensation,' ushering in a wholly new advance in communication with the spirit-sphere, is entirely without factual basis. So far from spiritism being anything new, it dates from the most ancient time."[2]

Unger cites the comment of G. Campbell Morgan that the word "medium," when it is used, can be substituted by the words "demonized man" or "demonized woman."[3]

The Bible is clear from its earliest revelation that all forms of divination and necromancy were contrary to God's will. For Israel, Jehovah was the only legitimate source to gain supernatural knowledge beyond man's grasp. God spoke through His representatives (cf., Deut. 18:10-19; Lev. 19:31; 20:6).

Many, who look upon psychic phenomena from a

scientific point of view, dismiss the concept of evil spirits and demons. They approach such phenomena as ESP, clairvoyance, telepathy and precognition as beyond normal scientific methodology. Questions for the Christian are: At what point, if any, is dealing with this phenomena a legitimate research into the hidden resources of reality? When does it become trespassing into enemy territory which is forbidden by God?

J. Stafford Wright, writing in *Eternity*, admits that, "On occasions individuals transcend the experience of space-time and bodily isolation, but these experiences are rare and cannot be forced. The Bible has room for them but nowhere encourages the Christian to cultivate them. A Christian who finds himself frequently experiencing second sight should be cautious and should pray much about it. As with any other gift, he should put into the hands of God for Him to use as He sees fit."[4]

While recognizing the reality of the unseen world and the validity of extrasensory perception, the Christian must beware of becoming involved and perhaps enamored with such things. As one prominent clergyman who claimed to make contact with the other side said, "The demonic is always very close."

In another *Eternity* article, J. Stafford Wright warns, "Christians cannot dabble with spiritualism without playing with fire. It is in the enemy-occupied territory. Christians must keep their hands clean even from the simple forms of spiritualism which, after all, merge into the higher forms. While there is no certainty that messages from individuals come from anyone other than the sitter and the medium, yet if any of them do, they must come from evil spirits."[5]

Merrill Unger pointed out that deceased people do not come back from the dead as spirits. The biblical teaching is that evil spirits impersonate the dead. The only case of a dead person ever returning as a spirit was when God permitted Samuel to speak to king Saul. In this case it was a "glaring exposé" of the falsity of spiritism. The medium's terror at the presence of a real spirit stands as good evidence of the fraudulency of her craft.

There is strong evidence, as observed by modern students of spiritism, that the "messages" from so-called "spirits" are really culled from the latent memories and subconscious feelings of those seeking messages from the departed. Perhaps these "insights" are extrapolated from the sitter through ESP, or some other form of "mind reading." This is not to deny that mediums can contact spiritual beings from the unseen world. The question is whether they do it all the time, and when they do, if such contact is with the actual departed spirit or an evil spirit.

The Christian has no doubts about the spiritual world, both good and evil, but he takes the biblical warnings seriously about contacting departed spirits. John Sutherland Bonnell ably presents the Christian view of seeking spiritual reality.

"The convinced Christian does not need a *medium* because he has a *Mediator*, who through spiritual communion makes the eternal world real to him. The Christian doctrine of the communion of saints has never been given its due. Through Christ we can have spiritual fellowship with those who have gone before. I firmly believe that the world of spiritual reality is not in some far-removed region beyond the stars but is truly 'closer . . . than breathing, and nearer than hands and feet.' To enter it requires no lengthy journey, only the opening of our eyes."[6]

WHAT DOES THE BIBLE SAY?

"Regard not them that have familiar spirits, neither seek after wizards, to be defiled by them: I am the Lord your God" (Lev. 19:31).

"When thou art come into the land which the Lord thy God giveth thee, thou shalt not learn to do after the abominations of those nations. There shall not be found among you any one that maketh his son or his daughter pass through the fire, or that useth divination, or an observer of times, or an enchanter, or a witch, or a charmer, or a consulter with familiar spirits, or a wizard, or a necromancer. For all that do these things are an abomination unto the Lord: and because of these abominations the Lord thy God doth drive them out from before thee" (Deut. 18:9-11).

"So Saul died for his transgression which he committed against the Lord, even against the word of the Lord, which he kept not, and also for asking counsel of one that had a familiar spirit, to inquire of it; And inquired not of the Lord . . ." (I Chron. 10:13, 14). (See I Sam. 28:1-25 for the story of Saul's experience with the medium at Endor.)

"And when they say to you, 'Consult the mediums and the wizards who chirp and mutter,' should not a people consult their God? Should they consult the dead on behalf of the living?" (Isa. 8:19 RSV).

"Wherefore I give you to understand, that no man speaking by the Spirit of God calleth Jesus accursed: and that no man can say that Jesus is the Lord, but by the Holy Ghost" (I Cor. 12:3).

"For there is one God and one mediator between God and men, the man Christ Jesus" (I Tim. 2:5).

"Now the Spirit speaketh expressly that in the latter times some shall depart from the faith, giving heed to seducing spirits, and doctrines of devils" (I Tim. 4:1).

"Beloved, believe not every spirit, but try the spirits whether they are of God: because many false prophets are gone out into the world. Hereby know ye the Spirit of God: every spirit that confesseth that Jesus Christ is come in the flesh is of God: And every spirit that confesseth not that Jesus Christ is come in the flesh is not of God: and this is that spirit of antichrist, whereof ye have heard that it should come, and even now already is it in the world" (I John 4:1-3).

" . . . for Satan himself is transformed into an angel of light" (I Cor. 11:14).

"Now the works of the flesh are manifest, which are . . . witchcraft . . ." (Gal. 5:19, 20).

"It is the spirit that quickeneth; the flesh profiteth nothing: the words that I speak unto you, they are spirit, and they are life" (John 6:63).

"God is a Spirit: and they that worship him must worship him in spirit and in truth" (John 4:24).

"But as it is written, Eye hath not seen, nor ear heard, neither have entered into the heart of man, the things which God hath prepared for them that love him. But God revealed them unto us by his Spirit: for the Spirit searcheth all things, yea, the deep things of God. For what man knoweth the things of a man, save the spirit of man which is in him? even so the things of God knoweth no man, but the Spirit of God. Now we have received, not the spirit of the world, but the Spirit which is of God; that we might know the things that are freely given to us of God. Which things also we speak, not in the words which man's wisdom teacheth, but which the Holy Ghost teacheth; comparing spiritual things with spiritual. But the natural man receiveth not the things of the Spirit of God: for they are foolishness unto him: neither can he know them because they are spiritually discerned" (I Cor. 2:9-14).

WHAT DO YOU SAY?

1. How do you explain the recent upsurge of interest in the spirit world and psychic phenomena?

2. How do you explain the prophet Samuel's appearance to king Saul when he consulted the witch of Endor (I Sam. 28:1-25)? What was the nature of that appearance? Did the medium actually cause Samuel's appearance? In what way is the story a repudiation of spiritism?

3. Why does God forbid consulting mediums and wizards? What motivation in seeking knowledge through a medium is contrary to God's revelation?

4. Is there a relation between demon activity and modern spiritism? Explain.

5 Is there a difference between participating in séances and communing with the spirit world and psychic research such as experiments with ESP and parapsychology?

6. Do you think people have a "gift of prophecy" today that enables them to see into the future (cf. I Cor. 12:10)? What do you make of recent predictions that have come true? Are such predictions simply good guesses?

7. In what ways does the present-day phenomena of psychic activity confirm the Christian claim of a supernatural spiritual world? Does it confirm the concept of life after death? How?

8. What are the dangers of experimenting with extra sensory perception, clairvoyance and fortune telling? (cf. I Chron. 10:13-14).

9. Why is it unnecessary for Christians to consult mediums? How is it a denial of God's revelation to us?

10. Why do modern spiritists deny that Jesus is the Son of God?

11. How do you explain such common feelings as: feeling you've been to a place before you visit there for the first time; getting a "hunch," or "feeling you're being watched" and finding it to be so?

12. Does Paul's reference in I Cor. 12:10 about distinguishing between the spirits refer to departed spirits? (Spiritists use this verse to justify their "discerning" the spirits.)

13. What is the difference between the "gifts of the Spirit" (I Cor. 12:1, 4, 7-11) and the claims of spiritism? What is the biblical test of a true spirit (cf. I Tim. 4:1)?

Notes

1. Jerome Ellison, "Arthur Ford and the Hereafter," *Christian Herald,* July 1968. Used by permission.

2. Merrill F. Unger, *Biblical Demonology,* pp. 157, 158. Copyright © 1955, Scripture Press Foundation. Used by permission.

3. *Ibid.,* p. 83.

4. J. Stafford Wright, "The Christian and Psychic Phenomena," *Eternity,* May 1968. Used by permission.

5. J. Stafford Wright, "The Christian and Psychic Phenomena," *Eternity,* June 1968. Used by permission.

6. John Sutherland Bonnell, "The Resurgence of Spiritism," *Christianity Today,* March 1, 1968. Copyright 1968 by *Christianity Today.* Reprinted by permission.

Should Science Tamper with Human Genes? 5

DETERMINING THE SEX OF AN UNBORN CHILD or being able to change the character of a child are not recent desires of geneticists. From ancient times man has looked for potions or tried witchcraft to accomplish these hopes. Galen, the personal physician to Roman Emperor Marcus Aurelius, told pregnant women to fill two small holes in the ground with urine. Plant wheat in one hole, barley in the other. If the wheat sprouted first a boy would be born; if the barley sprouted first, expect a girl. But Galen didn't invent the idea — archaeologists have discovered almost the exact formula on Egyptian papyrus written almost 4,000 years earlier.

Today's geneticists aren't influenced by witchcraft methodology. Rather, through a careful study of the chromosomes in an unborn child, they are not only able to tell maleness and femaleness, but far more important, to discover possible abnormalities. Serious study has also been given to possible links between abnormal chromosome arrangement and criminal behavior.

With the possibilities of eliminating forms of mental retardation, determining sex and even specifying sex by chromosome arrangement, treating children with chromosome abnormalities before they become potential compulsive criminals, and with the possibilities of developing a "super" race (since most genetic changes are irreversible from one generation to another) geneticists, the general public, political leaders, and the church are faced with some radical moral decisions.

Dr. Leroy Augenstein, former chairman of the department of biophysics at Michigan State University, stated:

"Since success in this area could allow us to control — for better or for worse — many other aspects of human life, the scientific developments and the ethical implications as well are particularly not only for individuals but for all of society.

"Each year I receive numerous inquiries from parents wanting to know the chances of their having an abnormal child. I cite one example. A couple wrote that their second child had been diagnosed as having cystic fibrosis; they wanted to know their chances of having another such child, as well as what dangers were in store for the offspring of their supposedly normal first child. We could give answers to both questions. CF is a so-called recessive trait, which means that children thus afflicted have two defective genes which are the cause of the condition; they receive one such gene from each parent. But in this case neither parent had CF; each had one good and one bad gene for this trait. Thus if they have additional children the chances at each pregnancy are one in four that the child will have two good genes, two in four that like its parents it will have one good gene and one bad gene, one in four that it will have two bad genes. That is, there is a 25 per cent probability that each future child will not have proper ligament formation and so will have trouble walking and using its arms and legs, that it will have seriously inadequate digestion, that it will have a large accumulation of fluid in its lungs, that it will be highly susceptible to infection, and that it will require at least $200 a month for medical assistance if it is to survive even into its teens.

"We can now give similar precise information for more than 500 physical defects. In some cases the repeat chances are one in four, but in others it may be one in two or one in three. Further, we can clinically test for 19 different recessive genes even before the first defective child is born. Unfortunately, these tests are not as refined as we would like; only in six or seven of them are we able to arrive at an answer almost every time. The tests to determine if a person has one good and one bad CF gene yield a definite answer in only about 60 percent of the cases.

"The major point to be made is that we are learning more and more about the unconceived child. In our society we believe — and, I think, properly so — that once a child is conceived it has the right, except in unusual circumstances, not to be aborted. Once a child is born it acquires all kinds of rights and privileges guaranteed by our laws — again, properly so. But an unconceived individual is a hypothetical nothing; it has no rights."[1]

Dr. Robert Edwards and Richard Gardner of Cambridge University's department of physiology say they have been able to remove rabbit embryos while still in the blastocyst stage, surgically remove some blastocyst cells for a test to determine sex, then replant only the blastocysts destined to develop into the chosen sex.

"The first application of the technique is likely to be found in animal breeding. Farmers building dairy herds don't want more than one or two male calves. The best beef, on the other hand, comes from males, so meat ranchers want only enough cows for breeding purposes. . . .

"Apart from the interest of ranchers and dairy farmers, the implications are obvious and enormous. If this procedure could be extended easily to man there might, for instance, be inbalances, even fads, in the selection by parents of one sex of child over another. Large inbalances in the ratio of men to women could strain society's seams, to put it mildly.

" 'The application of similar techniques to man is still remote', the researchers wrote in the May (1968) *New Scientist,* 'and depends upon solutions being found to the many problems still bedevilling attempts at the *in vitro* fertilization of human ova and the *in vitro* culture of human embryos. (A few workers report doing this, but others have not been able to duplicate their results.)'

"But once such problems have been solved, these techniques could be used to eradicate sex-linked diseases. When it becomes possible to determine the sex of human blastocysts with certainty, and also to identify quite certainly women who are (carriers of) a sex-linked disease, then it will be a simple matter to insure that no woman bears a male child.

"(Male children suffer the preponderance of sex-linked hereditary diseases. Further, for a disease as hemophilia to occur in a female the father must also have it, so that preventing birth of male hemophiliacs would eliminate the disease.)"

"Would not the non-replacement of a blastocyst, the researchers conclude, be socially and ethically far more acceptable than a full-scale abortion of the implanted, thriving fetus — the only alternative (to birth of diseased offspring) available today?"[2]

Studies of criminals reveal that a higher percentage have chromosome disorders than do people in the normal population.

"Sex in human beings is determined by two chromosomes which have long been designated X and Y; the normal female complement is XX, the normal male, XY. Whenever a newborn carries a Y chromosome he appears male, for it is the function of the Y chromosome to produce testes and ultimately male hormones. X and Y chromosomes have served mankind well as sex determinants, but they are by no means infallible.

"Once in every 500 male births, for example, the sex chromosome complement is XXY rather than XY, thus erring in the direction of femaleness. The resulting individual, called a Klinefelter male, is usually retarded, unusually tall and sterile.

"Erring in the other direction, however, is the XYY complement resulting in the 'supermale.' He is also unusually tall and somewhat retarded, but appears to be highly, perhaps too highly, sexually motivated. The XYY male is probably a rare creature, found once in 2,000 adult males at large, according to available surveys. From these two figures it can be estimated that one in 400 males or one in 80 tall males in the general population will carry either the XXY or XYY sex chromosome abnormality. . . .

"In 1962, William Court Brown of Edinburgh noted the predisposition of XXY males to larceny, fire-raising, and indecent exposure. . . .

"Dr. Court Brown's colleague, Patricia Jacobs, then pursued the matter one step further. In 1965, she performed chromosomal studies on 197 violently criminal Scots and found seven cases of XYY among them. Given an expected prevalence of only one XYY in 2,000 males, this experience was an eye opener and laid the groundwork for dozens of genetic investigations of criminals all over the world.

"One such study was carried out in our own cytogenetic laboratory at Elwyn Institute, a large private facility in suburban Philadelphia for the evaluation, education and rehabilitation of the mentally retarded. We were intrigued by Dr. Jacobs' contention that an extra Y chromosome results in tall stature, mild mental retardation and severely diordered personality characterized by violent, aggressive behavior. We therefore planned to confirm the extent of her studies.

. . . As reported in *Science*, we thus found a total of five XYY and seven Klinefelter males, all undiagnosed and all unsuspected, among 129 tall suspects. This resulted in an overall prevalence of one gross chromosomal error among each 11 tall criminal males rather than 1:80 as would be expected from chance alone. . . . Offenses listed in the records of these males included larceny, burglary, assult, attempted rape, rape, murder, sodomy, corrupt morals, prison breach and robbery. . . .

"It would seem that the XYY male is fast achieving similar stature. His symptoms, as we and other laboratories tend to think of them, are extremely tall stature, long limbs with striking long arm span, facial acne, mild mental retardation, severe mental illness (including psychosis) and aggressive, antisocial behavior involving a long history of arrests, frequently beginning at an early age.

"It should be made clear, however, that studies as these do not indicate that every criminal has a chromosomal error, or that every victim of a genetic mistake will turn to a life of crime."[3]

In an article in *Think*, the house organ of IBM, Mary A. Teller points out that "although Anglo-Saxon law made, as early as 1326, provision for defense by virtue of 'madness,' and epilepsy has been successfully used as a defense for murder in modern Britain, innocence by virtue of chromosomal constitution puts a new wrinkle in an ancient discipline. Furthermore, should a special biochemical cycle be revealed in XXY and XYY psychopaths — resulting in the periodic buildup of intolerable tension, as suggested by some case histories — the law will have to cope with pleas of 'irresistible impulse,' even when the defendant is fully aware of right and wrong and of the criminal nature of his act.

"The social dilemma has been well-stated by Judge Jerome N. Frank: 'Society must be protected against violence and at the same time avoid punishing sick men whose violence drives them beyond their control of brutal deeds. A society that punishes the sick is not wholly civilized. A society that does not restrain the dangerous madman lacks common sense.'

"One immediate and high-priority goal of this branch of medical genetics should be to promptly identify and treat, by the best means available, every carrier of a gross chromosomal error. To do less is a waste of our powers."[4]

Michael Hamilton, canon of Washington (D. C.) Cathedral, sets forth some of the moral considerations, both positive and negative, related to the geneticists' power to change the personalities and the potentials of people before they are born.

"Let me say at once that I believe we should take advantage of our new knowledge and powers and, with all the wisdom and courage we can muster, begin the process of genetic engineering. Let me say also that this opinion should not be equated with the teaching of any religious denomination. Until more theologians learn about the new genetic technology and sit down to discuss the issues with scientists, psychologists, lawmakers and others, formal pronouncements are at best premature. . . .

"The religious assumptions underlying my view stem from a theme which runs through the Old Testament and is especially evident in the Creation stories of Genesis, which state that God authorized man to have dominion over the natural world around him and, by implication, over his own body. This was not to be unrestrained authority; allied with it was man's responsibility to be a good steward of the material and animal world bestowed on him for his welfare. Again, the New Testament tells us that Christ used his powers to heal the sick and to subdue the elements, not for his personal advantage but as a means to further his ministry of servanthood. Finally, because the universe is the creation of a God who acts in love, because our world in spite of its famines and earthquakes is basically friendly to our existence, I would expect knowledge about that world, including genetic knowledge, to be of benefit to us. Of course, we may misuse knowledge and power — witness war and destruction — but as a Christian I still find ground for hope in God's benevolence and man's freedom. . . .

"If the technical problems involved in genetic interference to heal an individual or restore him to normality were not so great, a decision to interfere would be easier. Unfortunately, apart from the difficulty of its mechanics, we do not yet know what all the side-effects of such interference would be. . . .

"Another major genetic issue that faces us arises from so-called cloning. In the summer of 1968 two research scientists in Oxford, England, grew a frog from the nucleus of a single cell which had been removed from another frog. The new frog was identical with the first. Cloning is rather like planting a slip from a rose bush (the Greek word *klon* means 'slip') and growing a new bush from it. The frog operation is not always successful. To grow a human from a cell would certainly be much more difficult even if a slip were transplanted into a womb. But it is theoretically possible, and we may be sure that many experiments along these lines will soon be taking place around the world. By duplicating individuals we could have a hundred McCarthys or Wallaces, a hundred Walter Shirras or Carl Sandburgs. Think of the temptation to vanity to have a thousand copies of oneself made! But though these genetic duplicates would all look alike, each would develop a unique personality, because each would grow up in a different environment.

"I can see no *a priori* theological objection to human cloning if it were technically possible. . . .

"In my eyes, however, the concern that overrides

all others in this connection is that of the process by which decisions on these genetic issues will be made. The danger is that a policy regarding research or its application will be laid down privately by representatives of only one or only a minority of the social institutions that have a stake in the outcome."[5]

Canon Hamilton's final paragraph puts forth a challenge as to how a genetic policy ought to be formulated. At this level the Christian should become seriously involved so the best moral policy can be developed. Canon Hamilton says: "No one individual, profession or denomination, no one institution has the wisdom to discern the common good. The best policy will be discovered if we are willing to share with each other our separate experiences. Of course, the state and national legislatures will be the final arbiters of policy. They will establish the relevant laws and regulations and they will, directly or indirectly, fund most of the research determined on. They will give the nation the kind of policy it deserves. It behooves us therefore to take part in discussion and debate about genetic issues, so that their deliberations may be well informed and their decisions sound."[6]

WHAT DOES THE BIBLE SAY?

"And God said, Let us make man in our image, after our likeness: and let them have dominion over the fish of the sea, and over the fowl of the air, and over the cattle, and over all the earth, and over every creeping thing that creepeth upon the earth" (Gen. 1:26).

"For thou hast made him a little lower than the angels, and hast crowned him with glory and honor. Thou madest him to have dominion over the works of thy hands; thou hast put all things under his feet" (Ps. 8:5, 6).

"Jesus answered, and said unto him, Verily, verily, I say unto thee, Except a man be born again, he cannot see the kingdom of God. Except a man be born of water and of the Spirit, he cannot enter into the kingdom of God. That which is born of the flesh is flesh; and that which is born of the Spirit is spirit" (John 3:3, 5b, 6).

"Therefore if any man be in Christ, he is a new creature: old things are passed away; behold, all things are become new" (II Cor. 5:17).

"Being born again, not of corruptible seed, but of incorruptible, by the word of God, which liveth and abideth forever" (I Pet. 1:23).

"Train up a child in the way he should go: and when he is old, he will not depart from it" (Prov. 22:6).

"For the Lord giveth wisdom: out of the mouth cometh knowledge and understanding. He layeth up sound wisdom for the righteous: he is a buckler to them that walk uprightly. When wisdom entereth into thine heart, and knowledge is pleasant unto thy soul; discretion shall preserve thee, understanding shall keep thee" (Prov. 2: 6, 7, 10-11).

WHAT DO YOU SAY?

1. If we learn how to prevent or cure some genetically caused diseases, how much freedom should geneticists be given to make necessary genetic changes?

2. Why has the ability of geneticists to make genetic changes been labeled by some Christians as usurping God's power? What difference is there between making genetic changes and using other medical practices that alter a man's personality?

3. Could gene changing be classified somewhat in

the same category as organ transplants? Why? or why not?

4. If geneticists discover a way to raise children's I.Q.'s, should this be allowed?

5. When abnormal genetic structures that could produce either physical or mental deformity are discovered, what should be done knowing that changes are possible? Who should decide what should be done?

6. If further study of criminals reveals a greater percentage of those with chromosome disorders, should such people be held responsible for their criminal behavior? Should they be treated solely from a medical viewpoint?

7. If one of your children was discovered to have an XXY or an XYY chromosome disorder similar to those discovered in criminals, what would you do? How would you apply Proverbs 22:6 to this?

8. Can chromosomal caused disorders be altered by the conversion experience? How does the biblical teaching of regeneration relate to chromosomal behavior patterns?

9. What can be done to take the scare out of helpful and healthful genetic rearrangement? Why does the public often call it genetic manipulation?

10. What moral guidelines can the church offer the geneticist? How can the church help him fulfill such guidelines? Should such guidelines be put into laws? Would this limit the good effects of the geneticist?

11. In order to allow geneticists to be of greatest service to mankind, how can we counteract the "monster" theories that hinder genetic research?

Notes

1. Leroy Augenstein, *Changing Man: The Threat and the Promise,* edited by Kyle Haselden and Philip Hefner. Copyright 1969, Doubleday & Company, Inc.

2. Christopher Weathersbee, "Toward Preselected Sex," *Science News,* August 3, 1968. Reprinted with permission from *Science News,* the weekly news magazine of science and the applications of science, copyright 1968 by Science Service, Inc.

3. *Ibid.*

4. Mary A. Teller, "Are Some Criminals Born That Way?" *Think,* Nov.-Dec. 1968. Reprinted by permission from Think Magazine, published by IBM. Copyright 1968 by International Business Machines Corporation.

5. Michael Hamilton, "New Life for Old: Genetic Decisions," Copyright 1969, Christian Century Foundation. Reprinted by permission from the May 28, 1969 issue of *The Christian Century.*

6. *Ibid.*

How Free Are We to "Do Our Own Thing"? 6

EVER SINCE ADAM AND EVE asserted their freedom in the Garden of Eden, man has been expressing his freedom. Perhaps no other quality of man's existence has been so freely expressed and yet so little understood. Mankind has never been able to find the God-intended balance of recognizing His sovereignty and the reality of man's freedom without distorting one or the other. Philosophically man has either drifted toward a stifling determinism or toward an obsessive freedom. Politically he has wavered between tyranny and anarchy. On a personal level, man has bound himself either to restricting laws or flagrant libertinism. Throughout history the pendulum has often swung to the extremes.

Man in the latter part of the twentieth century finds himself wrestling with the problem of what freedom means and how far it extends. Today's youth question many of the traditions and laws handed down to them. In the name of freedom, they assert the right to "do their thing."

Modern technology has forced on contemporary man the necessity of a highly structured existence, mass produced goods and services, conformity, impersonal learning and depersonalized egos. The reaction to these things has been (perhaps a healthy one) a reassertion of individual freedom. Today's permissive society has allowed young people to experiment for themselves with things that other generations didn't have or that other generations felt the need to limit because of social pressures and moral restrictions. Today's young people freely use drugs, read all kinds of literature, (including pornography) experiment with sex (the pill has taken away the fear of pregnancy), and express their frustrations openly. Evidence of this is seen in protest movements, riots in the streets, antiwar mobilization and marches, modern fashions, nudity, the new morality, drug abuse, new concepts in music and art, and long hair on boys.

Perhaps in no other time in history have so many thought that they were completely free to do what they pleased. When such a condition exists there cannot help but be immense problems on both the psychological and sociological levels. Many things that are popular today have a "free" label attached to them — free speech, free love, free sex, free art, free expression. Freedom has become an obsession. Yet this freedom has little resemblance to the freedom sought by the American founding fathers and fighters for freedom. For many today, freedom means complete autonomy. It means "doing your own thing" without having any responsibility to anyone. It means unlimited self-expression regardless of how it affects others.

Prevalent attitudes of freedom center upon man himself. The idea of God's sovereignty no longer holds sway over men's minds. If there is no God, then man is supreme, autonomous, and morally free in every respect. Absolute laws have no meaning for the modern man who accepts the current popular atheistic philosophy. Though many tacitly accept these modern ideas, they have no moral convictions (even from a humanistic point of view) that prepare them, either intellectually or psychologically, to follow the logical conclusions of being completely autonomous. Under this philosophy man works out his problem

61

apart from divine aid. He seeks his own solutions to problems his freedom creates — alcoholism, drug abuse, suicide, venereal disease, mental disease and a host of other personal and social problems, from lung cancer to environmental pollution. Autonomous man has asserted his freedom, but how can he escape the results?

The very freedom men crave becomes the chain that enslaves. Modern ideas of freedom tend to thwart the true meaning of freedom. Robert C. Sproul in *Christianity Today* defines freedom as "the ability to choose (morally) what one wishes. Autonomy goes a step farther and says that an individual not only has the private ability to choose what is pleasing to himself but in so choosing is responsible to no one for his choice."[1]

Also in *Christianity Today*, Tunis Romein delineates between man's freedom and the claim to autonomy. He says, "The first word about man is that he is dependent, not that he is autonomous. The Creator endowed man with the glorious capacity of being free to answer yes or no, even to God himself, but man was in no sense endowed with the capacity of being non-answerable to his Maker. Man *must* answer yes or no to God and his freedom is contingent on this answer. To say no to God is to forfeit the very groundwork of human freedom, and to slip into the precipitous realm of the unfree, from which, humanly speaking, there is no recourse, just as when the eye is destroyed there is no recourse from physical blindness.

"The secular confusion about what really is the ground of freedom, and the disconcerting paradox involved in seeming to lose one's freedom in the act of pursuing it with great vigor, are counterbalanced with striking simplicity in the words of ancient Joshua: *Choose* (freedom) this day whom ye will *serve* (the other side of the freedom coin, from the biblical perspective). Freedom's cry for freedom in the name of man leads to an obsession about freedom, not to mention an eventual bondage. Freedom received within the context of obedience to the Eternal Word is true freedom; as it is written, 'If the Son therefore shall make you free, you shall be free indeed.' All of which is to say: Choose to be a slave in the right way and be free, or choose to be free in the wrong way and be a slave."[2]

Christians have been given the promise of freedom. Jesus said that if the Son makes us free we will be free indeed (John 8:36). The Bible speaks of all men as being sinners (Rom. 3:23). They have "turned, everyone to his own way" (Isa. 53:6). Jesus said that all who sin are the slaves of sin (John 8:34), and proclaimed that men could be free from their bondage only through Him. The New Testament presents the Christian as a free man, whose freedom is a valued and precious thing (Gal. 2:4; 5:1, 13; I Cor. 10: 29). But New Testament writers also warn against abusing the freedom we have as Christians (Gal 5: 13; I Cor. 8:9; I Peter 2:16).

Christian freedom is not the freedom to do what one pleases with no regard for the consequences. Two biblical principles stand out. First, our freedom is restricted by our relationship to God (I Peter 2:16; Matt. 22:37). God is the object of our love. This love for Him compels us to be His servants. Augustine, in effect, stated this principle when he said, "Love God and do as you please." Secondly, our freedom is also restricted by our relationship to others (I Cor. 8:9). As Christians we are concerned about how our actions affect other people. Even if we have a deep insight into Christian truth and are not bothered by such matters as whether meat was offered to idols (I Cor. 10:28, 29), we are to take into consideration the other person's viewpoint and "through love be servants to one another" (Gal. 5:13 RSV). Luther's famous statement perhaps sums up the Christian perspective: "A Christian man is a perfectly free lord of all, subject to none. A Christian man is a perfectly dutiful servant of all subject to all."

WHAT DOES THE BIBLE SAY?

"And the Lord God commanded the man, saying, Of every tree of the garden thou mayest freely eat" (Gen. 2:16).

"And I will walk at liberty: for I seek thy precepts" (Ps. 119:45).

"And ye shall know the truth, and the truth shall make you free" (John 8:32).

"Jesus answered them, Verily, verily, I say unto you, Whosoever committeth sin is the servant of sin. And the servant abideth not in the house for ever: but the Son abideth ever. If the Son therefore shall make you free, ye shall be free indeed" (John 8:34-36).

"All we like sheep have gone astray; we have turned every one to his own way" (Isa. 53:6a).

"Know ye not, that to whom ye yield yourselves servants to obey, his servant ye are whom ye obey; whether of sin unto death, or of obedience unto righteousness? Being then made free from sin, ye became the servants of righteousness. But now being made free from sin, and become servants to God, ye have your fruit unto holiness, and the end everlasting life" (Rom. 6:16, 18, 22).

"I find then a law, that, when I would do good, evil is present with me. For I delight in the law of God after the inward man: But I see another law in my members, warring against the law of my mind, and bringing me into captivity to the law of sin which is in my members. O wretched

64

man that I am! who shall deliver me from the body of this death? I thank God through Jesus Christ our Lord. So then with the mind I myself serve the law of God; but with the flesh the law of sin. For the law of the Spirit of life in Christ Jesus hath made me free from the law of sin and death" (Rom. 7:21-25; 8:2).

"For he that is called in the Lord, being a servant, is the Lord's freeman: likewise also he that is called, being free, is Christ's servant. Ye are bought with a price; be not ye the servants of men" (I Cor. 7:22-23).

"But take heed lest by any means this liberty of yours become a stumblingblock to them that are weak" (I Cor. 8:9).

"For though I be free from all men, yet have I made myself servant unto all, that I might gain the more" (I Cor. 9:19).

"All things are lawful for me, but all things are not expedient: all things are lawful for me, but all things edify not" (I Cor. 10:23).

"Now the Lord is that Spirit: and where the Spirit of the Lord is, there is liberty" (II Cor. 3:17).

". . . false brethren . . . came in privily to spy out our liberty which we have in Christ Jesus, that they might bring us into bondage" (Gal. 2:4).

"For, brethren, ye have been called unto liberty; only use not liberty for an occasion to the flesh, but by love serve one another. For all the law is fulfilled in one word, even in this; Thou shalt love thy neighbor as thyself" (Gal. 5:13, 14).

"As free, and not using your liberty for a cloak of maliciousness, but as the servants of God" (I Peter 2:16).

WHAT DO YOU SAY?

1. Why do we presently have so much emphasis on expressing one's freedom? What impels so many people to be "free" and "do their own thing"?

2. What safeguards are lacking in some modern uses of freedom and "doing one's thing"?

3. What is the difference between liberty and license? Between autonomy and liberty? Does freedom mean we can do whatever we want to?

4. Is there such a thing as absolute freedom? If so, what would be the effects upon individuals and society?

5. How does the abuse of freedom often lead to enslavement? Why does autonomy not always mean freedom in the true sense?

6. When the Bible speaks of the Christian possessing freedom, what does it mean? What did Jesus mean in John 8:36 when He said a Christian is one who is "free indeed"? How does truth make us free?

7. Did man have more freedom in the Garden of Eden before the fall than he did after he sinned? Explain.

8. How does the New Testament put restrictions on the Christian's freedom? What biblical principles guide Christians in their use of personal freedoms?

9. What endangered the freedom of Christians in New Testament times? Do Christians face the same type of dangers today?

10. How do legalistic tendencies among Christian

groups today restrict Christian freedom? What are some of the legalistic attitudes prevalent among Christians today?

11. In what sense can a Christian who serves God be more "free" than a non-Christian who claims no allegiance to anyone?

12. What did the Apostle Paul mean when he spoke of not having his liberty judged or determined by another man's conscience or scruples? (I Cor. 10:29 RSV).

Notes

1. Robert C. Sproul, "Existential Autonomy and Christian Freedom," *Christianity Today,* July 18, 1969. Copyright 1969 by *Christianity Today.* Reprinted by permission.

2. Tunis Romein, "Freedom: Possession or Obsession," *Christianity Today,* January 17, 1969. Copyright 1969 by *Christianity Today.* Reprinted by permission.

Is Your Church Responsible for Crime Prevention? 7

CRIME RATES CONTINUE TO SOAR. Since 1960, the yearly total of crimes has increased by 47 percent. Major crimes increased from 2 million to 3.7 million between 1960 and 1967 — an 88 percent overall increase. Crime is growing six times as fast as the country's population. Most law enforcement officials say we are at a crime crisis point.

What's so alarming about these statistics is the increase of major crimes against persons. Murders — up 40 percent; forcible rapes — up 60 percent; robberies — up 86 percent; aggravated assaults — up 66 percent; burglaries — up 80 percent. Auto thefts have doubled!

Various reasons are given for this steady increase in the crime rate: ghetto conditions, lack of modern police equipment, insufficient police personnel, court decisions that hamper police crime investigation, court leniency, racial radicals, permissiveness in families, breakdown of family life.

U. S. News & World Report in August 1966 included what they called *a deeper cause*:

"Nearly every official agrees that the causes of the crime problem lie deep in the American society — and that the final answer to the problem is not to be found in more police or better courts.

"'Public attitude' is blamed for causing crime to get out of hand.

"'A spirit of lawlessness' and a 'contempt for law'

are said to be growing among American people.

"'A breakdown in family life' is cited. Parents are blamed for failing to discipline their youngsters.

"'Moral values' are described as deteriorating.

"'Civil-rights leaders' are accused of contributing to contempt for law by telling Negroes that they have a right to disobey laws they consider unjust.

"'Violence' is seen to be gaining wide acceptance as a way for people to express frustration and resentment.

"Riots are viewed as a natural product of all this.

"The police command of Taylor [Assistant Chief Inspector Harry Taylor of New York City Police] includes the Negro ghetto of Harlem. Perhaps nowhere else in the U.S. is there a greater concentration of crime problems. Here is how Mr. Taylor describes what he calls the 'national crisis in crime' and its causes:

"'Here in New York City, you can see how the crisis becomes more inflamed, year after year.

"'But it isn't just a New York crisis. It's a national sickness. Every big city in the U. S. is infected.

"'I'm not talking about organized crime. What I'm talking about is "unorganized" crime — the kind that touches everybody and jeopardizes the safety of people in the streets, in their homes, and their places of business. That's where the national crisis lies.

"'In many cities, women are afraid to go to work after dark. And they have good reasons. Rapes, assaults, sadistic outbursts of senseless violence are on the rise. Crimes often seem to be committed out of sheer savagery.

"'This is something new in American life.

"'Respect for law and order is declining!' "

Former U. S. Attorney General Nicholas Katzenbach released a rather interesting report on crime entitled *The Challenge of Crime in a Free Society,* which unfortunately received little attention. It brings balance into the situation:

"Among the findings of the survey were these: (1) only one-third of all burglaries are reported to the police; (2) there are 50 percent more robberies than are reported to the police; (3) forcible rape is the crime least likely to be reported; (4) one-third of the people surveyed stated that they believe it is unsafe to walk alone at night in their own neighborhood; (5) slightly over a third stated that they kept firearms in the house as protection against criminals. The commission was careful to point out, however, that the problem of 'crime in the streets' often is exaggerated. In two-thirds of the cases of willful homicide and aggravated assault and in one-half of the reported cases of rape, the criminal and the victim are acquainted. Robbery is the one form of violence in which the assailant usually is a stranger to the victim. . . .

". . . in 1965 only one out of eight reported major crimes was a crime of violence; the other seven were thefts of one form or another, and burglary accounted for three out of these seven. Further, the commission stressed the fact that the economic . . . loss of property [does] not begin to approach the economic losses caused by white collar crime — embezzlement, labor racketeering, price-rigging, tax evasion, bribery, graft, loan sharking and fraud. . . .

"In a time when the American people are increasingly disturbed over random acts of violence in the streets, they continue to show a high level of tolerance for the Cosa Nostra and its allies. . . .

"Most incidents of violent protest and most crimes against persons and property involve boys and young men. In 1965, persons under age 25 committed three-fourths of the nine major types of crime against persons and property — robbery, burglary, theft, petty larceny, motor vehicle theft, willful homicide, negligent homicide, forcible rape, aggravated assault. The

15-24 age group is the most crime-prone group in our population. . . .

"More and more Americans are coming to believe that violence is the only alternative left to those who seek social and economic justice for the poor, a greater degree of participation in the decision-making of our society's public and voluntary organizations and institutions, and fundamental changes in the nation's foreign policy."[2]

Invariably, when the law and order theme enters a discussion on crime, Americans polarize. Law and order has become the badge of many who want to maintain the status quo. And those of the militant minority have concluded that law and order is simply a moralistic slogan for further suppression. Unfortunately, both of these conclusions have some factual basis in our society.

Perhaps one of society's biggest hang-ups in finding an adequate solution to crime is its unwillingness to admit that crime is a moral problem. Treating the surface causes without getting to the heart of the problem — the need for changed individuals — cannot remedy the situation on a permanent basis. It may only alter the types of crimes that are committed. When sociologists, as well as theologians, place responsibility upon the individual for criminal behavior, then perhaps we'll begin to make more progress toward reducing crime in our society.

"For decades sociologists have argued that crime is an illness not a sin, that criminals do not freely choose a life of larceny, prostitution or narcotic peddling. They have become criminals because society deprived them of the normal childhood and education in which moral principles are acquired, and denied them opportunities to satisfy their basic needs legitimately. In other words, society itself has been viewed as the primary source of anti-social behavior. In recent years, however, some social scientists have begun to attack this assumption, and to go beyond it to inquire just how free men are to set their own course, how responsible they are for their conduct, as measured against the extent their behavior is controlled by social, economic, and cultural conditions. . . .

"In *Delinquency and Drift* (1964) David Matza extends his analysis of delinquent behavior to argue that while some men are freer than others, all of them have a significant measure of freedom: there are choices to be made, alternative norms of behavior to adopt — or to combine, as is often the case, by drifting from one to another. To support this position, he draws on evidence which has often embarrassed sociologists, that people who come from the same neighborhood, culture, even gang, eventually lead quite different lives; thus, their future, in some part, depends on what they themselves make out of their past and their opportunities."[3]

Along with this necessity of accepting responsibility for one's deeds is the necessity of self-limitations of activities. While desiring liberty to act as one pleases, one must not turn liberty into license that infringes upon the rights of others.

"In all parts of the world, a surging concern for the extension and preservation of human rights has been accompanied by a general decline in public morals. People sneer at restrictions and demand more and more freedom. Their taste of liberty and their dislike for restraint causes some to go from liberty to license. They abuse freedom, disregard the rights of others, and exceed their own rights by breaking the rules of conduct laid down by the majority.

"If civil rights mean anything they mean the inviolability of the dignity of man, which requires that other people refrain from molestation and violation. . . .

"Crime and violence defile human dignity. People who try to make us believe that no change for the better can come about without blood and fire and illegal tumult of all kinds are profoundly ignorant of the meaning of our democracy. Democracy cannot survive if society chooses to be apathetic to lawlessness and disorder. Such neglect can lead only to anarchy. . . . Anarchy is a disavowal of law and government, a brutish life which would destroy the cohesive material that holds a society together and gives it stability."[4]

While community leaders, civil rights advocates, and politicians have attempted to find solutions to the crime problem, many churches have done little or nothing. Often local churches have avoided involvement. They reason that if crime is the result of sin, the crime problem will vanish only when mankind deals with the sin problem. Unfortunately, many churches have done little to help men find adequate solutions to sin problems. A generalized preaching against sin isn't the answer.

In most large cities, churches have simply moved to the suburbs as a way of circumventing crime and racial problems. From the suburban vantage point, it is easier to pontificate a "law and order" gospel.

Lyle Schaller, director of the center for parish development, Evangelical Theological Seminary, Naperville, Ill., speaking for the more liberally oriented churches, says, "It can be said without exaggeration that the biggest single threat to the growing interest in church renewal in America is the rising level of violence and fear of violence. Once again survival bids fair to replace service as the dominant objective of the parish.

"In the 1950s, racial justice became the number one concern of the churches. In the 1960s, with the rediscovery of poverty, 'race and poverty' became the dominant issues in the nation's religious circles. In the 1970s, the problem will be further enlarged as crime and violence are added to the list of the churches' most urgent concerns. . . .

"If the churches, by their action or inaction, condone a repressive policy of law and order during the next few years, the consequences likewise will be felt in every part of the nation (including the supposedly safe all-white suburban or rural community)."[5]

From another viewpoint, Donald R. Davis states: "Granted, then, that we all want law and order, what can we do in the present to find it? One obvious thing we must do is maintain order. This is the function of government (Rom. 13:1) and is recognized as such by the *Report of the National Advisory Commission on Civil Disorder* (the Kerner Report). The report says, 'Preserving civil peace is the first responsibility of government. Unless the rule of law prevails, our society will lack not only order but also the environment essential to social and economic progress.'

"Let us be a people of law and order. Evangelical Christians are committed to this by the teaching of Scripture. But let us also remember that we are committed by the Scriptures to justice and neighbor-love. Let us therefore be a people who participate in government, not to protect just our own rights, but the rights of others. This is the best way to preserve the rule of law and maintain order."[6]

While the most common response to the crime problem may simply be to avoid it, this hardly can be the Christian approach. Crime prevention must become the responsibility of the church if the church is to be a champion to preserve the rights of all people.

WHAT DOES THE BIBLE SAY?

"Thou shalt not follow a multitude to do evil; neither shalt thou speak in a cause to decline after many to wrest judgment: Neither shalt thou countenance a poor man in his cause" (Ex. 23: 2, 3).

"Ye shall not steal, neither deal falsely, neither lie one to another. And ye shall not swear by my name falsely, neither shalt thou profane the name of thy God: I am the Lord. Thou shalt not defraud thy neighbor, neither rob him . . ." (Lev. 19:11-13).

"The people of the land have used oppression, and exercised robbery, and have vexed the poor and needy: yea, they have oppressed the stranger wrongfully. And I sought for a man among them, that should make up the hedge, and stand in the gap before me for the land, that I should destroy it: but I found none" (Ezek. 22:29-30).

". . . For the Lord hath a controversy with the inhabitants of the land, because there is no truth, nor mercy, nor knowledge of God in the land. By swearing, and lying, and killing, and stealing, and committing adultery, they break out, and blood toucheth blood. Therefore shall the land mourn, and every one that dwelleth therein shall languish . . ." (Hosea 4:1-3).

"Let him that stole steal no more: but rather let him labor, working with his hands the thing which is good . . ." (Eph. 4:28).

"But he that doeth wrong shall receive for the wrong which he hath done: and there is no respect of persons" (Col. 3:25).

"Brethren, if a man be overtaken in a fault, ye which are spiritual, restore such a one in the spirit of meekness; considering thyself, lest thou also be tempted. Bear ye one another's burdens, and so fulfill the law of Christ. For if a man think himself to be something, when he is nothing, he deceiveth himself" (Gal. 6:1-3).

WHAT DO YOU SAY?

1. Why does the Bible have so much to say about the punishment of crime? Why was prescribed punishment usually severe? (Cf. Lev. 20:10-18, Deut. 13:6-11.) Are evangelical Christians influenced too greatly by Old Testament practices?

2. Should we work first toward securing social, economic and racial justice before stressing law and order? If we did this, do you think we would need to stress law and order at all?

3. Why does our society condemn the more obviously violent crimes and seemingly condone other types of crime (such as: embezzlement, petty thievery, etc.)?

4. Has the evangelical segment of the church been reluctant to institute sociological programs for the prevention of crime? Why?

5. What constructive methods toward crime prevention can the church adopt to help reduce crime?

6. In what ways can a local church cooperate with law enforcement officials?

7. Should the church take some of the blame for the increased crime in the nation? Why or why not?

8. What is being done to rehabilitate criminals in your county? Can the church participate in such programs as an expression of the gospel's ability to alleviate men's problems? Explain.

9. If the gospel is the ultimate answer to man's personal needs, how can it be applied to situations that breed crime?

10. How can the church help reverse some of the causes of crime mentioned by law enforcement officials and sociologists? What is your local church doing in this respect?

11. What has your church done or what is it presently doing to bring released prisoners into a Christian environment?

12. Should employers make an effort to hire released prisoners in an effort to rehabilitate them? Do you know of any that are doing this? How effective are they?

Notes

1. *U.S. News & World Report,* "Crime Wave — What Can Be Done About It?" from a copyrighted article in *U.S. News & World Report* of August 1, 1966.

2. Lyle E. Schaller, "Crime, Violence and the Local Church." Copyright 1969, Christian Century Foundation. Reprinted by permission from the May 7, 1969 issue of *The Christian Century.*

3. "Respect for the Law," *The Royal Bank of Canada Monthly Letter,* Vol. 50, No. 3, March 1969. Used by permission.

4. Amitai Etzioni, "Crime and Free Will," *Book World,* October 30, 1966. Used by permission.

5. Schaller, *Respect for the Law.*

6. Donald R. Davis, "Who's for Law and Order?" *The Other Side* (formerly *Freedom Now*), Nov.-Dec. 1968. Used by permission.

Sex Education – Why Not? 8

SEX EDUCATION HAS BECOME an explosive and divisive issue. Communities have become arenas of bitterness and hatred over a subject that is supposed to have its essential roots in love. The controversy rages over what is being taught, how it is being taught, and who is teaching it. Yet, while opposition to sex education is quite vocal and organized, a recent Gallup poll indicated that 71 percent of Americans favor having sex education taught in the public schools.

People oppose aspects of sex education programs in schools for various reasons. The most publicized opposition recently has been inspired by far right organizations such as the John Birch Society and the Christian Crusade. An article in *Reader's Digest*, by Carl T. Rowan and David M. Mazie, aptly summarizes the right-wing views and approach: "The Christian Crusade, founded by Billy James Hargis in 1947, specializes in promotions of conservative causes via radio, TV and pamphlets. It first focused on sex education early in 1968, after Gordon V. Drake became its director of education. Drake's pamphlet, called 'Is the Schoolhouse the Proper Place to Teach Raw Sex?,' has become the bible of sex-education fighters, and Drake has become their No. 1 spokesman. He tours the country, sometimes appearing at half a dozen rallies a week to help organize opposition to sex education. A Drake rally blends God, patriotism and homespun values with emotionalism and eye-catching examples to shock the audience. Arms waving and fingers wagging, the short, animated Drake charges, 'They've thrown God and the Bible out of school and put sex education in.'

"The Birch Society discovered the subject last winter, identified it as a 'filthy communist plot,' and called all Birchers to conduct 'organized, nationwide, intensive, angry and determined' opposition to sex education in public schools. Their campaign has attracted other right-wing support, including that of the Virginia branch of George Wallace's American Party. Although the ties that bind all these groups and individuals together are vague, there is no doubt that cooperation exists and is increasing. The same material appears in city after city; the same techniques and arguments are used across the country."[1]

All over the country people have risen in opposition to sex education in the schools. Groups with catchy titles are aggressive in their fight. In New Jersey they call themselves PAUSE (People Against Unconstitutional Sex Education); in California, POSE (Parents Opposed to Sex Education); in Iowa and Idaho, POSST (Parents Opposed to Sex and Sensitivity Training); in Oklahoma, SOS (Sanity on Sex); in North Dakota, PAMS (Parents Advocating Morality Standards); in Texas, AVERT (Association of Volunteers for Educational Responsibility in Texas). These and other groups with acronym titles are growing all over the country. Their main target is an organization that also has become known by its abbreviated title, SIECUS, (Sex Information and Education Council of the United States).

SIECUS was founded in 1964 on the principle that health education, including complete information on sex and family life, should be taught systematically in public schools, beginning in kindergarten and going up through high school. The organization itself does not control what material is used in the schools, and in fact advocates local control of sex education programs. Dr. Mary Calderone, the executive director of SIECUS is the primary target of many who oppose the kind of sex education advocated by SIECUS. She is outspoken and some of her statements are used against her by SIECUS opponents. One ultraconservative spokesman called her "the biggest serpent of them all," for making such statements as, "by the age of ten, a child should master the factual aspects of reproduction." While she comes far short of teaching biblical ethics, she does emphasize the need for honesty and responsibility between boys and girls.

SIECUS has also been criticized for its alleged association with a magazine called *Sexology*, which is considered pornographic by its critics. It contains articles written in a professional and factual manner. Isadore Rubin, editor of the magazine, refused to answer questions before the Senate Internal Security Subcommittee concerning his alleged communist affiliation, and this has hurt SIECUS. The effectiveness of SIECUS has been weakened considerably because of all the controversy it has generated. Its identification with those whose viewpoints and life style offend Christian people, its association with *Sexology*, and the high turnover of its board members have made the organization suspect in the eyes of many.

Perhaps too much emphasis has been placed on organizations and personalities and not enough on the need for constructive sex education in school curriculum programs. Robert T. Coote said in *Eternity*, ". . . the Far Right decries the very idea of sex education in the schools. But we believe there are good reasons for authorizing the schools to help parents and society in this vital area, providing the program is carefully prepared and wisely presented. Virtually every major educational, medical, and governmental organization concerned with youth has endorsed sex education, and we see no good reason for evangelicals to flatly oppose it. There are questions that can be raised — indeed that should be raised by Christian parents — but some program of sex education makes sense in this day and age, and Christians should recognize this."[2]

Not all the criticism of sex education is attributable to extreme conservative groups. People with moderate views have spoken out against the cure-all promises of some sex education advocates and against excessive and erotic approaches (one teacher was dismissed because she encouraged students to kiss, fondle and express themselves as they saw fit). Many believe that children can be irreparably hurt by learning too much too soon. They cite the Freudian theory of "latency" during the years of 6 through 11. During this time the child's sexual impulses are sublimated to other pursuits. Thus they do not need graphic portrayals of sex information. Such frankness and objectivity could cause more harm than good.

Harold Lindsell said in *Christianity Today,* "Critics have been quite justified in expressing disapproval of graphic materials that depict chickens, dogs, and human beings engaged in the sex act. Unless sensitive teachers offer further explanations, this type of presentation implies that intercourse is merely an animal act. It is indeed a physical activity that satisfies a normal appetite; but it is much more than this, and a child is cheated when the sexual relationship is not presented in a context of love, personal concern, the giving of self, and the concept of moral choice.

"Moreover, children should be taught the facts of life only when they are old enough and mature enough to accept them without psychological harm or undue embarrassment. Even teen-agers do not need to be given detailed information about all aspects of the sexual relationship. Some things can wait for the post-high school years and the approach of marriage.

81

Sex is a very personal and intimate matter, and those who feel the urge to tell all in the supposed interest of candor and honesty should remember that the law of love may transcend candor and honesty at this point. Not all inhibitions are bad."[3]

Others disagree, and believe our open society, which presents raw sex in magazines, movies and on TV, makes it necessary to counteract with explicit teaching on sex matters in order to prepare children for the emotional shocks of sex as it is presented in our culture. Dr. W. T. Tompkins, an obstetrical consultant to the U. S. Children's Bureau, said that we need the "fourth R — reproduction." It should be taught objectively and factually and not related to sex in itself. It should be taught to prepare children to react favorably in situations where sex and psychological problems interact to develop emotional trauma. The theory seems to be, the more facts you know the less hang-ups you will have. But this idea has yet to be proven. Until such proof is available, this idea cannot be accepted too readily.

Unwittingly, these controversies may produce more good than we think. They have aroused people to take a keener interest in the whole subject of sex education, and even in other aspects of their children's development.

Christians, who have ignored this issue in the past, are taking a broader interest, and are now asking what they can do to make sex education a workable and acceptable concept in public schools. Most Christians recognize the importance of sex education in the home, but they have not yet realistically come to grips with it in the church and in the public school. Now they are roused to action. But there is need to give constructive direction to school boards, rather than simply offering narrow criticism. Christians do not have to accept everything local schools propose concerning sex education, but they must guard against fighting it for the wrong reasons. Appealing to "communist plots," engaging in character assassination and presuming guilt by association will not bring about the kind of atmosphere that will foster healthy education about reproduction and family life. There are positive things Christians can do that will avoid bitterness and antagonism.

Dr. John Scanzoni, associate professor of sociology at Indiana University, points to some things Christian parents can do. He says; "First they should go to PTA and school board meetings where family life education (FLE) is the topic and help shape and approve material to be used in each grade. For example, a great fear of some parents is that young children will be exposed to 'too much too soon.' However, even young children today gather enormous misinformation from their peers. Far better that parents and schools decide together what is appropriate for a certain age level and provide accurate information to counteract peer influence.

"Second, and far more crucial than curriculum, is the teacher. There are currently very few people qualified to handle FLE courses, especially at the junior high and senior high school levels. Therefore, Christian parents should personally know who is going to teach these courses. They should request the right to interview him before he is hired, to assess his qualifications and his views. . . .

"Third and most vital of all is what the parent does in the home. If he transmits clearly the dynamic of Jesus Christ as applied to all areas of male-female relationships, there is virtually nothing to be feared from any outside influence."[4]

Harold Lindsell stresses the role of the church and parents. He says, "Christian parents should see that their churches provide sex-education classes as part of the Christian education program. Churches can help parents also by offering instruction for them as well as for their children. Evangelical Sunday school publishing houses have an opportunity and a responsibility to make materials for sex education available. . . .

"Ultimately the kind of education that children receive can be determined by the parents. If their children are given what they disapprove of, they have no one to blame but themselves. Human nature, marred by sin, stands in need of correction, and sex education will never be any better than the people who control it. Therefore eternal vigilance by parents is the price of adequacy, purity, and biblical soundness in sex education — a highly important need ideally fulfilled by a properly functioning program involving the home, the church and the school."[5]

Scripture places the responsibility for training and instructing children in the home. It does not divide education into "facts" and "moral truth." Training is an integrated whole, fact and truth are not separated. No aspect of living, whether it is sex, work or worship, is separated from the other; all come under the loving relationship toward God, with all one's heart, soul, mind and strength.

WHAT DOES THE BIBLE SAY?

"And thou shalt love the Lord thy God with all thy heart, and with all thy soul, and with all thy mind, and with all thy strength: this is the first commandment" (Mark 12:30).

"And these words, which I command thee this day, shall be in thine heart: And thou shalt teach them diligently unto thy children, and shalt talk of them when thou sittest in thine house, and when thou walkest by the way, and when thou liest down, and when thou risest up" (Deut. 6:6, 7).

"Train up a child in the way he should go: and

when he is old, he will not depart from it" (Prov. 22:6).

"The rod and reproof give wisdom: but a child left to himself bringeth his mother to shame" (Prov. 29:15).

"And, ye fathers, provoke not your children to wrath: but bring them up in the nurture and admonition of the Lord" (Eph. 6:4).

"Wives, submit yourselves unto your own husbands, as it is fit in the Lord. Husbands, love your wives, and be not bitter against them. Children, obey your parents in all things: for this is well-pleasing unto the Lord. Fathers, provoke not your children to anger, lest they be discouraged" (Col. 3:18-21).

"But continue thou in the things which thou hast learned and hast been assured of, knowing of whom thou hast learned them; and that from a child thou hast known the holy Scriptures, which are able to make thee wise unto salvation through faith which is in Christ Jesus" (II Tim. 3:14, 15).

"Unto the pure all things are pure: but unto them that are defiled and unbelieving is nothing pure; but even their mind and conscience is defiled" (Tit. 1:15).

"But if you call yourself a Jew and rely upon the law and boast of your relation to God and know his will and approve what is excellent, because you are instructed in the law, and if you are sure that you are a guide to the blind, a light to those who are in darkness, a corrector of the foolish, a teacher of children, having in the law the embodiment of knowledge and truth — you then who teach others, will you not teach yourself? . . . You who say that one must not commit adultery, do you commit adultery? . . ." (Rom. 2:17-22 RSV).

"And the things that thou hast heard of me among many witnesses, the same commit thou to faithful men, who shall be able to teach others also" (II Tim. 2:2).

WHAT DO YOU SAY?

1. Why should the question of teaching sex education in schools be a matter of Christian concern? Should sex education classes be voluntary or mandatory in public schools?

2. Should parents be responsible for *all* of a child's sex education? Does the biblical command to "train up a child," include sex education?

3. What can parents do to guarantee that sex education programs in public schools are properly administered and taught?

4. Can sex education be taught in a factual and neutral way, without moral responsibility being stressed? Is moral training the job of the school?

5. Is there a certain age when children should be taught about human reproduction? What are the dangers of learning "too much too soon"? Should a child be given more information than he asks for? When? When not?

6. How do parents' actions and attitudes toward each other relate to a child's sex education? How does the emotional tone and the tenderness and respect of husband and wife in the home affect a child's attitude toward sex?

7. Sex educators believe that greater and more accurate knowledge of sex among young people will help prevent sexual misconduct. Has this been proven? Do you think it can have the opposite effect? How can increased knowledge be of value?

8. What are the dangers of not telling children the truth to such questions as, "where did I come from?" and "how did the baby get inside you?"

9. Are there benefits in being frank and honest? What are the dangers? Should we "tell all"? Are some inhibitions good?

10. Why do many parents hesitate to talk freely about sex matters to their children? Why do some parents tell false stories about reproduction and childbearing? Does this stem from the idea that "sex is bad"?

11. Should churches have sex education classes? Who should teach them? What age levels should be taught?

12. What are the dangers of making sex education in schools an ideological question? Have extreme groups helped or hindered the cause of good sex education?

13. How can Christians help counteract the poor image given to evangelical Christianity by certain conservative religious organizations who have helped stir up bitter controversy over sex education?

Notes

1. Carl T. Rowan and David M. Mazie, "Sex Education: Powder Keg in Our Schools," *The Reader's Digest*, October 1969. Used by permission.

2. Robert T. Coote, "Sex Education: Where to Now?" *Eternity*, November 1969. Used by permission.

3. Harold Lindsell, "Sex, SIECUS, and the Schools," *Christianity Today*, January 30, 1970. Copyright 1970 by *Christianity Today*. Reprinted by permission.

4. John Sconzoni, "Should We Fear Sex Education?" *Eternity*, November 1969. Used by permission.

5. Lindsell, *op. cit.*

Do We Need New Concepts of Missionary Outreach? 9

DESPITE THE MULTIPLIED USES of electronic technology and scientific development, Protestant Christians are falling pathetically behind in the struggle for the hearts and minds of Earth's millions. Ratio-wise, the Protestant population remains the same as it was 130 years ago. World population has tripled, yet the Protestant population remains at 8 percent. If the population explosion continues at the present rate for the next 30 years, Protestants will only claim 2 percent of the world's people.

According to Missionary Research Library, North American Protestant missionaries abroad have reached an all-time high of 33,270. Nearly $300 million is the present annual expenditure — a 75 percent increase in 10 years. Evangelicals account for nearly 70 percent of the personnel and 45 percent of the giving. Unfortunately, evangelicals have spread their personnel through a multitude of agencies, causing considerable waste of talent and funds.

Olan Hendrix, home secretary for the Far Eastern Gospel Crusade, states: "There are simply too many foreign mission organizations today. These result in excessive overhead expense, duplication of effort, and confusion in the minds of the public.

"We need to begin investigating the possibility of combining some of our organizations. In the directory of the North American Protestant Foreign Mission

Agencies, 427 mission organizations are listed. In the International Foreign Missions Association there are 47 mission organizations with 8,413 missionaries and home staff members. Twelve organizations with IFMA have 200 or more missionaries and comprise 73 percent of the total missionary and home staff population. The other 35 organizations make up the remaining 27 percent of the personnel. Thirty-five groups have fewer than 200 workers each, and 16 groups have fewer than 50 workers.

"Not long ago a missionary conference was held at a Bible institute in Western Canada. A score of mission boards were invited to come, present their needy fields, challenge young people to volunteer as candidates to their particular areas, distribute thousands of pieces of literature, and show dozens of films and filmstrips.

"From one major city alone, eight missionary deputation workers independently drove their cars 1,500 miles to reach the school, each lugging a movie projector, each with a trunk packed with mission literature. On the way, all eight bought the cheapest lunches and stayed overnight in low-priced motels, in order to conserve the Lord's money.

"But no one seemed to consider the larger waste of the Lord's money — the needless overlap of personnel, of equipment, of promotional materials, of transportation costs.

"And so scores of mission boards compete daily with each other, reaching into the same hip pockets for funds, speaking in the same schools for candidates, and displaying their wares in the same churches for support.

"Some mission boards are too small to do an adequate work in candidate recruitment. Others have no trained personnel to produce adequate mission publications. Still others have no trained businessmen to make their home offices work smoothly and efficiently.

"And so the proliferation of missions causes both an extravagant duplication of effort, a confusing competition between the vast variety of mission boards, and a lack of efficient handling of the home office."[1]

While many people propagate the idea that the world is continually closing to mission efforts, no less than 138 nations allow Christian missionaries into their countries. Yet in these nations, over one million cities and towns have no resident missionary.

Traditional missionary approaches — including preaching, teaching, and direct evangelism — still dominate the concepts and practices of most present-day missionaries. Much missionary work is still being done in the hinterland — away from the teeming cities, away from the cultural centers, away from the large numbers of college students who will become the future leaders of the countries, and away from the upper-class people who are in control of the countries. Too often the missionary is still pictured traveling through dense jungles with a Frank Buck hat. Missionary Roger Schrage gives the perfect example:

"When speaking of Brazil, many people get a mental picture of the Amazon rain forest and naked Indians eking out a living from the river. Perhaps a missionary from there comes through their home church and tells heart-rending stories of sickness, cruelty and death. This plucks the heartstrings and so out comes the money, and the equipment and the personnel. Certainly these places and needs exist. But let us examine the situation a bit and see if they hold the priority they are given.

"Hundreds of personnel and thousands of dollars are being poured out to reach less than 80,000 Brazilian Indians. Yet I can take you to a Brazilian city that has a population greater than that with no missionary. There are, however, four national pastors.

In this city we find 90,000 people that speak one language and the whole Bible is in that language. There are three radio stations on which time can be bought very cheaply. There is a ready acceptance of the gospel, but where are the personnel and funds to buy up the opportunity? Can it be that they are being spent translating the Bible into a tongue that will soon be dead?

"I am not against evangelizing the Indians or others in rural areas. What I ask is *do we not have the same obligation to the millions that are flooding the cities?*

"But city work does not have the romantic glow over it that work in the jungle has — at least not for the church back home. The hardships of survival in the jungle sound much more like missionary life than a traffic jam in the city. When a missionary dies in the hands of savages, the whole world honors him as a hero. But what of the missionary that dies in a multi-car accident on a four-lane Brazilian highway?"[2]

Developing nations aren't looking for back-in-the-jungle type missionaries who only want to convert people from their former religions. These countries are demanding that we send doctors, nurses, teachers, agriculture experts, engineers, and those with special skills to help people help themselves to a better life. They want personnel who do more than bring Westernized religion. They want help in agriculture, economics, sociological, and cultural development. If missionaries can help in these areas, they are welcomed with open arms. If they can't, they can be assured that more countries will soon reject all missionaries. This will not be persecution because of the missionaries' faith, but simply because they did little to help develop the people within the countries.

C. Peter Wagner, assistant director of Andes Evangelical Mission, and director of Emmaus Bible Institute, Cochabamba, Bolivia, makes these observations:

"One of our chief weaknesses, as one observer humorously put it, is that we have tended to regard our neighbor as 'a soul with ears.' Evangelistic passion is a virtue, but can become a stumbling block if not held in balance with the scriptural view of the whole man. Some missionaries seem to look upon the people in the land where they minister only as potential converts. Human beings are regarded as means to an end (building the church of Christ) and not as ends in themselves. Where this psychology exists, the inevitable result is paternalism, perhaps the most despised missionary attitude in the eyes of the younger churches. . . .

"Evangelicals have excelled in training spiritual pastors and evangelists on the Bible institute level, and these dedicated workers are now the backbone of many a national church. But there has been a certain reluctance to develop the full potential of future leaders, raising them to academic levels equal or superior to those of the missionary.

"There is perhaps a subtle 'great white father' complex in all of us. We say piously that missionaries should be working themselves out of their jobs, but do we really mean it? . . . The soul-with-ears syndrome begins with a legitimate concern for the salvation of a man's soul but at times carries with it a devastating lack of concern for his material being . . . .

"There is another very subtle evangelical attitude which might also be traced to this paternalism. This is the strong appeal to the exotic, the steaming jungle, the naked savage to our homeland constituency. Savage Indians are photogenic, they furnish reams of material for prayer letters and they have no difficulty accepting the missionary as their great white father. . . . When it is decided to fly missionary converts from Ecuador to the Berlin Congress, the choice is not a converted Communist in the University of Quito but the savage Auca Indians. . . .

"The savages must be reached to fulfill the Great Commission, but is our overall missionary enterprise properly balanced in view of the teeming Christless masses in the world's metropolitan centers?

"Though our theological convictions may not change, our methods of communicating them must. What does the Bible say in regard to the cosmic implications of Christ's redemption? Is salvation of a community possible, or is it strictly an individual matter? Could God condemn a person to hell simply because that person had never heard the name of Christ in his lifetime? In what sense is Christ Lord? . . .

"Christian social action should not be thought of as providing the entering wedge for the gospel. Missions which have introduced social institutions with the idea of building churches on top of them have generally been disappointed. The cart was before the horse. But even more common is the fallacy that one can measure the success of a social action program in terms of souls saved. If the Lord gives souls as a result of social action, fine, but this should not be the chief end. The chief end of this ministry is to improve the lives of people in the community in which it works.

"Christian social action must follow evangelism. This is an imperative. A born-again believer who does not feel a burden for the social well-being of his neighbor comes under the judgment of Scripture."[3]

In the areas of recruitment and training, the demand for better equipped missionaries also demands rethinking. Gone are the days when anyone with zeal and a Bible school diploma could consider himself fully trained to minister "to the natives." Now that more men and women of considerable skills are available for short term service and many times willing to pay their own way, new types of missionary opportunities are available.

Jack F. Shepherd, former chairman of the department of missions, Nyack Missionary College, Nyack, N. Y., says, "Missionary training can be contemporary — within our present structure and programs — if we examine them with scrupulous honesty and work on them with energetic creativeness. I believe it is better to revise and revive present structures than to hastily dismiss them as obsolete with only theoretical constructs as replacements. . . . Two fundamental problems confront any proposal for change in missionary training. The first is the incredible range of activities and functions which can be classified under the category of 'missionary.' Does any other vocational specialization gather under one name such a varied collection of job descriptions? The only thing that gives commonality to the whole business is the 'sending' process. . . .

"A baffling array of schools and institutions of missions are conducted to train and orient this wide variety of people. If those who direct these programs are alert to the need for creative change and enjoy the confidence and support of the agencies which they serve when they introduce this kind of change, our missions may indeed begin to meet current needs. . . . To make missionary training contemporary does not require new areas of study, but rather new dimensions within these areas. . . .

"We need to broaden our theology into new dimensions. A narrow theological interpretation can severely limit one's biblical perspective. There is a kind of relativity to theology that makes broadness essential and beneficial. Our theologies need to be rephrased under constant judgment of the Word as they are related to new worlds of thought and language. . . .

"We need to lengthen our geographical dimensions in missions. Flags, maps, costumes and the like have been colorful attractions to strengthen deputation presentations. But in our day, when there is a more intimate understanding of the world, this approach not only becomes ineffective, but it is in danger of becoming offensive. . . .

"A penetration beyond theory and ideal to actualities and real issues might come if our training programs provided for direct contact with prejudice, poverty, discrimination and oppression in the context of a prospective missionary's own land and culture — not just on the foreign field where it may be identified as something common to 'them' and not to 'us.' This might help to relieve him of that tendency toward a cultural and national sense of superiority that so often limits acceptance of missionaries."[4]

Short term missionary service helps fulfill many needs. Raymond Prigodich, a Conservative Baptist missionary appointee asks, "Is lifetime commitment an essential prerequisite to foreign missionary service? Traditionally, mission boards have thought so. But 20 years ago experimentation began with a new departure in the missionary enterprise — short-term service abroad.

"Short-term service may involve a stay as short as two weeks or as long as five years, but its essential feature is that once the term is completed, the volunteer is free to return to his normal routine at home. . . . The advent of the Peace Corps in 1961 stimulated expansion of existing short-term programs and led several additional mission organizations into the field. . . .

"How widespread is this new trend? Sudan Interior Mission recently queried more than 100 missions. Of the 51 that responded, 22 currently use short-term volunteers, four others have used them but no longer do so, 22 consider this new venture impractical and the remainder are still open on the subject. Of the groups which have sent out short-termers, most have thus far used fewer than 100. . . .

"SIM's Raymond J. Davis notes that short-term service is not a substitute for, but a complement to, lifetime service, adding that 'almost anything that is being done today to earn a living at home may be usefully employed on the mission field.' "[5]

As these new approaches are tried and proven in churches throughout the United States, especially as the youth of today grow up into leadership positions in the churches, there will be an increasing call for missionary strategy to make corresponding changes. These changes are long overdue. Happy will be the mission board that prepares today for new approaches to present the gospel throughout the world. Keeping up with the times in both approach and analysis in the countries which a mission board operates, will increase the success of reaching people for Christ.

WHAT DOES THE BIBLE SAY?

"And this gospel of the kingdom shall be preached in all the world for a witness unto all nations; and then shall the end come" (Matt. 24:14).

"Go ye therefore, and teach all nations, baptizing them in the name of the Father, and of the Son, and of the Holy Ghost: Teaching them to observe all things whatsoever I have commanded you: and, lo, I am with you alway, even unto the end of the world." Amen (Matt. 28:19, 20).

"Sing unto the Lord, all the earth; show forth from day to day his salvation. Declare his glory among the heathen; his marvelous works among all nations" (I Chron. 16:23, 24).

"And he gave some, apostles; and some, prophets; and some, evangelists; and some, pastors and teachers; For the perfecting of the saints, for the work of the ministry, for the edifying of the body of Christ" (Eph. 4:11, 12).

"As every man hath received the gift, even so minister the same one to another, as good stewards of the manifold grace of God" (I Pet. 4: 10).

"But, beloved, we are persuaded better things of you, and things that accompany salvation, though we thus speak. For God is not unrighteous to forget your work and labor of love, which ye have showed toward his name, in that ye have ministered to the saints, and do minister" (Heb. 6:9, 10).

"And as ye go, preach, saying, The kingdom of heaven is at hand. Heal the sick, cleanse the lepers, raise the dead, cast out devils: freely ye have received, freely give" (Matt. 10:7, 8).

"But ye shall receive power, after that the Holy Ghost is come upon you: and ye shall be witnesses unto me both in Jerusalem, and in all Judaea, and in Samaria, and unto the uttermost part of the earth" (Acts 1:8).

WHAT DO YOU SAY?

1. What kind of missionary work do you believe is the most profitable in winning people to Christianity? Can missionaries rightfully engage in social ministries that do not have direct evangelistic thrusts? Why or why not?

2. In what ways can missionaries make greater use of technological advancements?

3. Why should missions engage in limited outreaches — such as translating the Bible into a language spoken by only 5,000 — when nearby multitudes are barely being reached?

4. How can missionaries avoid superimposing Amer-

ican culture on people in other countries? How can they best serve the national churches?

5. How can the less glamorous mission activities, such as school teaching, be presented in challenging ways to a missionary's supporting constituencies? Would you fully and enthusiastically support some less glamorous mission activities? Name some.

6. Why is missionary outreach often a neglected ministry of local churches? What place should missions have in a local church program?

7. Is there a missionary shortage in your denomination? Why? What can be done to recruit more candidates?

8. Are requirements for missionaries in your church too stringent? Are these in keeping with the rising educational standards around the world?

9. Should more missionaries be placed in urban centers and fewer in rural mission work? What does your mission board do to win college students on foreign fields?

10. What is the basic philosophy behind short-term mission service? What benefits are derived — for the mission, for the participant? Is this plan wise from the viewpoint of using available people and funds? Is lifetime commitment to missionary service necessary?

11. Is supporting small mission agencies a wise investment of funds and personnel, considering the amount of overhead expenses and the limited training programs such missions can offer? Could these missions operate more efficiently if they merged with other boards?

12. Why are many small missions so reluctant to merge with other missions? Should supporters force such mergers? Why or why not?

Notes

1. Olan Hendrix, "Too Many Missions?" *Eternity*, April 1966. Used by permission.

2. Roger Schrage, "But Where Are the Lions?" *Eternity*, April, 1966. Used by permission.

3. C. Peter Wagner, "Reshaping Missions," *World Vision Magazine*, May 1967. Used by permission.

4. Jack F. Shepherd, "Let's Make Missionary Training Contemporary," *World Vision Magazine*, Nov. 1969. Used by permission.

5. Raymond Prigodich, "Wanted: Missionaries, 2 weeks to 5 years," *Eternity*, March 1969. Used by permission.

How Should Christians View the Use of Drugs? 10

MODERN DRUGS AND THE SCIENCE OF PHARMACOLOGY have done wonders for the relief of illness and pain. Drugs are a necessary part of modern life. Millions of people would suffer needlessly if we did not have a vast knowledge of drugs that will kill pain or rehabilitate diseased tissue. Few would want to live in a world where they could get no relief from pain, especially if that relief could be had through properly administered drugs. The dangers of using drugs, however, are not always evident. Many people unwittingly get "hooked" on habit-forming drugs that were intended to be used only in small dosages or for short periods of time. Some people who get "turned on" soon find that they cannot get "turned off." Taking pills that alter one's mental state is an easy way to escape life's problems. An easily-taken pill seems so much less an evil than facing the realities of life, which often force one to deal with intricate, often frustrating, interpersonal relationships.

The use of mind-altering drugs, including excessive alcohol, amphetamines, barbiturates and tranquilizers, is widespread. An editor of *The New York Times* estimated that about 100 million Americans use such drugs. National polls show that at least 20 percent of the prescriptions written in the United States are for mind-altering or mood-changing type drugs. These figures clearly indicate that the drug problem is not limited to the so-called hard drugs such as heroin or morphine. They include the common drugs which are easily obtainable through prescriptions at local drug stores. The question of misusing drugs touches not only the addicted, but anyone who uses drugs. Experts speak of "drug dependence" as well as drug addiction.

The World Health Organization defines drug addiction as "a state of periodic or chronic intoxication produced by the repeated consumption of a drug (natural or synthetic)." The characteristics of addiction include: (1) an uncontrollable desire and need to continue taking a drug and to get it by any means; (2) a tendency to increase the dose; (3) a psychological and physical dependence on the effects of the drug; (4) a detrimental effect on the addict and society.

The *Royal Bank of Canada Monthly Letter* reminded its readers that not everyone uses common sense when it comes to drugs: "Drugs are used by people who feel small in the face of the complexities of life, by people who seek a temporary feeling of importance, by people who wish to depress their anxiety or to raise their spirits, or by people who desire to experience hallucinations. It is this unnatural self-indulgence that is the damaging use of drugs."[1]

Drugs can produce a variety of effects on people. Some drugs (caffeine, cocaine, amphetamine), can combat fatigue, some (alcohol, barbiturates, morphine), can raise a person's mood; others banish worries (alcohol, tobacco, morphine, meprobamate, barbiturates); induce sleep (barbiturates, chloral hydrate, alcohol); and cause dreams (morphine, cocaine, marijuana, mescaline, lysergic acid-LSD).

Many are alarmed about the excessive use of drugs. They have sought the reasons for the increase in drug abuse. Research has found that many, regretfully, get hooked through ignorance. Other contributing factors — the temper of the times, the breakdown of family life, social unrest, the threat of annihilation, youthful independence and rebellion — add to the complexity of the problem.

Time states, "As with any social habit, all kinds of people use drugs for all kinds of reasons. One obvious age-old drive is the simple impulse to feel good. Like the neolithic men who got high on fermented berries and the Assyrians who sucked opium lozenges, explains Dr. Sidney Cohen of NIMH, a noted drug researcher, today's drug takers 'are bored, in pain, frustrated, unable to enjoy, or alienated, and some plant or substance carries with it the promise of oblivion, surcease, quietude, togetherness, or euphoria.' Says one Chicago college student who smokes marijuana regularly: 'You take it when friends get together or when you're going to see *Yellow Submarine*. It's not to solve problems, just to giggle.' "[2]

Drug abuse by young people is a problem of enormous proportions. In their anxiety to cope with the restrictions of established society, young people are falling into an enslaving conformity of their own. Experimentation with drugs is considered an "in" thing. Youth considers getting high on "pot" no more harmful than adults taking a cocktail before dinner or a drink of wine before sleeping. Great differences of opinion over the real effects of marijuana have been advanced. Since little long-term research has been done, many take a very permissive attitude toward it. They say we should treat it as we do alcohol: make it available and legal.

Those who support legalizing marijuana point out that present laws are based on outmoded ideas about drugs, which confuse "hard" drugs with nonaddictive ones. They point out that smoking tobacco has been proven more dangerous to health than smoking marijuana. A team of researchers at one university concluded, after studying over 100 marijuana users, that

102

using pot was not harmful to them, but actually helped them. These researchers said that those who used drugs showed a keener awareness of their surroundings and had a better understanding of human nature.

David Wilkerson, who has worked with drug addicts for several years in his Teen Challenge centers, and who has interviewed thousands of drug users, takes strong issue with present permissive attitudes. He says, "I disagree totally with the current permissive attitude toward marijuana. *I consider marijuana the most dangerous drug used today.* . . .

"What the 'experts,' who think they know all the answers don't know is this: *90 percent of all the drug addicts we have ever treated began with marijuana and then graduated to something harder.*

"I can tell you from firsthand experience that marijuana users become just as 'hooked' as persons addicted to heroin. Chronic marijuana users lose their motivation and develop antisocial tendencies which often lead to violent antisocial behavior.

"I know what marijuana does. It breaks down resistance to drugs. It paves the way to alcoholism and drug addiction. It destroys moral values, especially sex standards."[3]

Dr. James L. Goddard, former director of the U. S. Food and Drug Administration, also agrees that marijuana should not be legalized. He wrote in *Life*, "I do not believe that marijuana should now be legalized, and the steps which I have suggested will not satisfy those who seek to legalize it. Their arguments are that the laws are not enforceable, that the use of marijuana is a private act and does not harm society, and that marijuana is less a danger than alcohol. These are attractive arguments but they begin to break down upon closer examination. First, although not precisely defined, law may have a deterrent effect. Second, although the use of marijuana is a private act, it has the potential to cause harm to society. One only has to visualize marijuana being more freely available and more widely used by adolescents who have not learned to cope with the problems of daily life, and it is not difficult to reach the conclusion that cannabism would become a societal problem. Our inability to keep cigarettes away from minors should serve as a reminder that we would not be able to keep marijuana out of their hands.

"I know that my stand on marijuana may seem contradictory. If the *known* harmful effects of alcohol and tobacco are greater than those of marijuana, and those substances are legal, why do I not advocate legalizing marijuana? I believe that if alcohol and tobacco were not already legal, we might very well decide *not* to legalize them — knowing what we now know."[4]

Another disturbing phenomenon in the present drug scene is the use of LSD (lysergic acid diethylamide) to produce a religious experience. Dr. Timothy Leary, a former Harvard professor, has advocated LSD as a "sacrament" to help a worshipper become "turned on." By using LSD the person takes a "trip" into mystical heights and sees visions. It alters one's perspective and supposedly helps people see the other side of things. The drug undoubtedly has fantastic effects on the human mind, but not necessarily predictable ones. These effects are far from religious.

Lambert Dolphin, who experimented with LSD before he became a Christian, describes his experience: "Shortly after taking these drugs I began to experience heightened audio and visual perception. Background music became ecstatically alive and full of living richness. The musical instruments became spatially deep and vividly alive inside of me. Vivid color patterns and fantasies in three dimensions filled my mind when I closed my eyes, and with open eyes I perceived the objects in the room with amazing depth, clarity and a shimmering, crystalline glow. Gradually I lost awareness of my body and seemed to be pulled ever deeper downwards into the past and into myself. Strange emotional experiences and long forgotten dreams bubbled up inside.

"I had the feeling that I was outside myself, looking from a new perspective into thousands of corridors of my life as if I were a whole universe in miniature. At times I seemed to be a vast cathedral. I was aware of history and the past as neither gone nor inaccessible. Time became strangely distorted and I even experienced the terrible sensation of time stoppage and endless eternity.

"Unpleasant and terrible fears associated with conception, birth, and early childhood gripped my mind and for painfully long periods of time I was caught up in closed cycles of temporary insanity and terrible vast worlds of unreality. The environment around me became strangely alive and hauntingly familiar.

"Strange forces and powers seemed to seethe about me, calling and pulling at my soul. And I was aware of the remoteness of God who seemed far off and inaccessible. It did not occur to me to pray. Instead I wondered who I was and how I would ever find myself."[5]

The widespread use of drugs, from the "junkie" trying to escape from life's problems to the "acid head" straining for a satisfying religious experience, challenges the church to present a vital answer to the groping emptiness of modern life. The "life expanding" qualities of the biblical message are often missing in the local church. The uninvolvement of Christians in the real problems of people is a primary cause for young people to seek "kicks" through drugs. Young people want life that is vibrant and vivid. Too often they find emptiness. They must be shown that Christ can fill the emptiness and void that modern life breeds. Until then, many will seek substitutes.

"Blessed are they which do hunger and thirst after righteousness: for they shall be filled" (Matt. 5:6).

"Oh that men would praise the Lord for his goodness, and for his wonderful works to the children of men! For he satisfieth the longing soul, and filleth the hungry soul with goodness" (Ps. 107:8, 9).

"Therefore I say unto you, Take no thought for your life, what ye shall eat, or what ye shall drink; nor yet for your body, what ye shall put on. Is not life more than meat and the body than raiment?" (Matt. 6:25).

"Be careful for nothing, but in every thing by prayer and supplication with thanksgiving let your requests be made known unto God. And the peace of God, which passeth all understanding, shall keep your hearts and minds through Christ Jesus" (Phil. 4:6, 7).

"They gave him vinegar to drink mingled with gall: and when he had tasted thereof, he would not drink" (Matt. 27:34).

". . . I am come that they might have life, and that they might have it more abundantly" (John 10:10).

"But whosoever drinketh of the water that I shall give him shall never thirst; but the water that I shall give him shall be in him a well of water springing up into everlasting life" (John 4:14).

"I beseech you therefore, brethren, by the mercies of God, that ye present your bodies a living sacrifice, holy, acceptable unto God, which is your reasonable service. And be not conformed to this world: but be ye transformed by the renewing of your mind, that ye may prove what is that good, and acceptable, and perfect will of God" (Rom. 12:1, 2).

"For the kingdom of God is not meat and drink; but righteousness, and peace, and joy in the Holy Ghost" (Rom. 14:17).

"All things are lawful unto me, but all things are not expedient: all things are lawful for me, but I will not be brought under the power of any" (I Cor. 6:12).

"What! Know ye not that your body is the temple of the Holy Ghost which is in you, which ye have of God, and ye are not your own? For ye are bought with a price: therefore glorify God in your body, and in your spirit, which are God's" (I Cor. 6:19, 20).

"Let no man beguile you of your reward in a voluntary humility and worshipping of angels, intruding into those things which he hath not seen, vainly puffed up by his fleshly mind. And not holding the Head, from which all the body by joints and bands having nourishment ministered, and knit together, increaseth with the increase of God" (Col. 2:18, 19; see Col. 2:8-13; 3:1-3).

WHAT DO YOU SAY?

1. What should the Christian's attitude be toward using tranquilizers and barbiturates to help relieve tension and bring rest or sleep?

2. What are the dangers of taking sleeping pills and tranquilizers? Should they ever be taken without a doctor's advice?

3. What factors in modern living have made the use of drugs so widespread and acceptable?

4. Can aspirin and other simple "pain-relievers" be harmful? Is there a difference between taking aspirin for relief of a headache or other minor pain and taking marijuana just to feel good? If so, what is the difference?

5. Why do drugs like marijuana appeal to young people today? What elements in training children and young people will protect them from drug misuse? What kind of drug education should be given to children? When and where?

6. Should marijuana be legalized? Is it any worse than alcohol? Is the argument that marijuana is less harmful than tobacco or alcohol a valid one? What would the effects of legalization be?

7. Does the use of marijuana necessarily lead to addiction to more potent and dangerous drugs? If not, what are some other dangers? How do drugs keep people from facing the realities of life? In what ways are drugs poor substitutes for coming to grips with one's problems?

8. Assuming LSD does bring a person to heightened experience and greater sensitivity to reality, what does such an experience fail to do? Could LSD produce a genuine religious experience according to biblical standards?

9. What in the Christian message implies that drug taking is a poor substitute for a personal experience with God? In view of these truths, do Christians need drugs?

10. For what reasons, if any, should Christians use drugs? Should Christians avoid using certain drugs? What can Christians do to help those who misuse drugs? How should Christians view the drug addict?

Notes

1. Misuse of Drugs: Some Facts," *The Royal Bank of Canada Monthly Letter,* September 1968. Used by permission.

2. "Pop Drugs: The High as a Way of Life," *Time,* September 26, 1969. Reprinted by permission from *Time,* The Weekly Newsmagazine; Copyright Time Inc. 1969.

3. David Wilkerson, "Should Marijuana Be Legalized?" *The Church Herald,* March 15, 1968. Used by permission.

4. James L. Goddard, "Should It Be Legalized? 'Soon We Will Know,' " *Life,* October 31, 1969. Used by permission.

5. Lambert Dolphin, Jr., "A Trip with LSD," *His,* March 1967. Reprinted by permission from *His,* student magazine of Inter-Varsity Christian Fellowship, © 1967.

Are Demons Real Today? 11

MODERN PSYCHIATRY HAS REJECTED the idea that demons are real. They have explained all abnormal behavior as an emotional disturbance of one kind or another. Anyone who would insist that such disturbances are possibly caused by evil spirits invading the personality of a human would himself be considered a case for psychiatric treatment.

Likewise, modern theologians have thoroughly poohpoohed the concept that demons are living, spiritual beings who have powers beyond human powers. Theologians have interpreted all the demonic references in Scripture to be cases of emotional illness — often citing modern psychiatric diagnosis as proof. Demythologizers have simply labeled such references to demons as unscientific superstition. Even some Roman Catholic theologians have argued for an abolition of demonology, which is interesting in the light of the long history of Catholic beliefs about witches and demons and its stringent punishment to those who practiced sorcery or witchcraft.

For many years evangelicals, who proclaimed the existence of demons, made such proclamations with tongue in cheek. They sought to be biblically sound, yet also desired to be up-to-date. Thus, for many evangelicals demonism only occurred in uncivilized countries, not in civilized societies. While this idea is still prevalent, there has been much interest shown in reports of actual demonic activity in advanced countries.

While psychiatry and modern theology continue their denial of demonism, based mostly on a rejection of biblical statements, demonism seems to be showing its ugly head more frequently. The following are some recent examples that are difficult to refute.

Evangelical Alliance Mission French worker Arthur Johnston reports: "I was not far from the Opera House on the Boulevard des Italiens and noticed a group of people standing in a circle. . . . Sitting in a chair, blindfolded, was a young lady about 25 years of age. Her hands were covered by a small rug, and she was writing feverishly. In a moment I realized that she was a clairvoyant and that she was selling written answers to questions asked her about personal affairs by people in the group. A man who was her accomplice was collecting the money.

"When interest in the fortune-telling routines seemed to wane, the man took a five-franc note from a person in the crowd and asked the blindfolded girl to tell what serial numbers were on the money. She recited the numbers without hesitation. Then he asked the girl for the license numbers of automobiles passing on the street behind her. She 'read' the numbers accurately as he pointed to the automobiles — though it was obviously impossible for the blindfolded girl to see them or to get signal in any way from her accomplice.

"Finally the man took a book from one of the students who stopped to watch the amazing girl. He opened it at random and asked the girl to 'read' the words in the page before him. As she recited the highly technical material, the astonished student confirmed the fact that she was quoting the book, word for word. . . .

"Standing at the edge of the circle I prayed, 'Lord, if this young lady has some evil supernatural power,

111

I pray in the name of Jesus that You will confuse the spirit and cause her to lose this power.' I also hastened to ask for protection for myself as God's child in the presence of unseen 'principalities and powers.'

"Immediately after I prayed, the girl's accomplice took a book from a student and asked the girl what was written on the page to which he opened it. She seemed tongue-tied and unable to answer. Obviously confused, the man then said, 'Well, try this page.' Again, she was unable to 'read'. He asked for another book from one of the other students. This also proved a complete frustration to the girl. Her power — at least for the moment — was gone.

"As I walked away, I thanked the Lord quietly that He had enabled me to see with my own eyes the nature of the spiritual battle in which we are engaged in France."[1]

Another TEAM missionary gives this report of an experience in Rhodesia: "On the floor of the solitary confinement cell two African women faced each other stoically. One was a white-haired grandmother; the other a younger mother of six children. Their crime was murder. Brutally and senselessly, they had slain a little child to appease the spirits of their ancestors.

"The simple bush women looked more like innocent children than murderesses as they sat together, resigned to their punishment of life imprisonment.

"It was a story that is all too familiar among the primitive people of Africa. The rains were poor and the ground showed little prospect of producing enough food for their families. Starvation was a very real possibility. As they watched their crops wither, the two women decided to consult with the local witch doctor. He offered an immediate diagnosis and a positive remedy.

"The spirits of their ancestors had been angered. They were withholding the rain until they were appeased. This demanded a human sacrifice — the death of a one-year-old child who must also be a relative. Confident that this would end the drought, the women murdered a little boy and brought to the witch doctor the organs he demanded for his heathen ceremony of appeasement.

"To their honest surprise, they were arrested, charged with murder, convicted, and sent to prison for life."[2]

Eternity editor, Dr. Russell T. Hitt, has been studying demonology for several years. He took a cautious view of the subject because so many reports seemed outlandish. Thus, when he wrote on the subject, he checked out the reports before printing them. Even though these verified accounts seemed weird, they led Dr. Hitt to give a strong affirmation to the biblical teaching that demons existed. The following are several of the verified cases reported by Dr. Hitt:

"Early in 1969 poltergeist phenomena (rapping and movement of objects without traceable human cause) were reported in the home of Sylvio Saint Onge in Quebec. Four priests investigated the strange happenings, including a statue of the Virgin that fell and broke for no apparent reason, a picture of Our Lady of Perpetual Help that was constantly thrown to the floor despite a very solid nail holding it, clothing that left the closet and gathered in the center of the room and the foot of a bed which would rise in the air and then fall to the floor. The investigators concluded: 'The Devil, if God allows it, can manifest himself tangibly by all sorts . . . of pesterings of certain people or things, as happened in the lives of many saints.'

"And, in London an Irish-born Dominican, F. Basil Prendergast, was suspended from his teaching post after reportedly indulging in witchcraft and the black mass. He was accused of taking part in nude rites and meetings of a witches' coven. Most serious charge against him was that he had been seeking a virgin to participate in the black mass. . . .

"But perhaps more unbelievable in this age of scientific achievement and sophistication is the real-life story of 17-year-old Bernadette Hasler, a pretty Swiss girl who was beaten to death May 14, 1966, because she was charged with incubus (lying with an evil spirit during sleep). This weird case came to light at the Zurich trial of a defrocked German priest and five of his followers, who were charged with murdering Miss Hasler while trying to exorcise a demon from her.

"Christian workers in Switzerland have reported that there is scarcely a village in that beautiful country that does not have a 'witch' or medium who casts spells or brews potions in the manner of their medieval predecessors. There are reportedly 2,000 mediums in Zurich alone. . . .

"Kermit Zopfi, while director of the German Bible Institute, encountered a youth named Rolf who expressed a desire to become a Christian. As Zopfi knelt by the side of a bed to pray with the young man, the missionary felt the bed shaking. He opened his eyes to find Rolf trembling violently as though he had convulsions. He began gasping for air as though he were choking, then flung himself on the bed.

"Then Rolf cried out, 'The Devil will not let me pray. I belong to him.' Later it was discovered that Rolf's father was a leader of a devil worship cult. Rolf himself had participated in a ceremony committing his life to the Devil. Some months later Rolf was able to accept Christ and turn from his life of bondage."[3]

Ray B. Buker, Sr., Professor of Missions, Emeritus, at Conservative Baptist Theological Seminary, Denver, Colo., after getting firsthand reports of several instances of demon possession encountered by his missionary son in West Pakistan, makes these observations:

"These incidents indicate that demon possession was not limited to the first century. It is found among primitive people today. Other cases could be cited among the tribes of Yunnan, the Indians of Latin America, and the Bantus of Africa that establish the fact that there is demon possession in the twentieth century.

"These events occurred in primitive societies. That demon possession is prevalent in such an environment will be accepted by most knowledgeable people. There is, however, serious scepticism as to the occurrence of such manifestations in a more sophisticated society where civilization has developed higher levels.

"Yet Raymond Frame . . . narrates an experience here in America in the twentieth century which clearly illustrates the fact of demon possession in our society. Jill was an attractive, mature 18-year-old Christian. Popular in high school, her bright appearance and warm nature quietly won her a good position. But it also got her into trouble; she went to bed with the man for whom she worked. Her sin preyed upon her mind and in due time she developed the symptoms of insanity. She became dangerous, threatening her Christian friends with physical harm. A physician consigned her to a mental institution.

"When Frame visited in the community in the course of his deputation tour he was told about the case. Because of his experience in China with demon-possessed people he recognized it as such and so diagnosed it. He called concerned Christians to prayer. Frame left the next morning. When he returned a year later he learned that the girl had been delivered the day of the prayer intercession. After she served the probation period in the institution, she entered a Bible school and eventually married. She is now the mother in a very fine Christian home.

"We do hold that demon possession is prevalent today even in the midst of our sophisticated society. The expressions are without doubt many and extremely varied. From Scripture we are aware that Satan is intelligent. He must not be considered in terms of his manifestations in biblical times. Whereas he will always be the arch-enemy of God and Christ, the cultural conditions have changed. He must disguise his activities in the forms of the present day life. We can therefore expect him to function in a clever and shrewd manner. . . .

"There is the impression among some that Satan and demons as persons, manifesting themselves through and in human beings, is a thing of the past. The assumption is that demon activity ceased in the first century. This we must reject. The Scriptures nowhere teach this. The picture in the New Testament is of an increasing contest, a battle, a war between Satan and the believer until Christ finally comes as the conqueror and binder of Satan and his angels. Until then Satan is the present Lord of this world."[4]

WHAT DOES THE BIBLE SAY?

"And when he was come to the other side into the country of the Gergesenes, there met him two possessed with devils, coming out of the tombs, exceeding fierce, so that no man might pass by that way. And behold, they cried out, saying, What have we to do with thee, Jesus, thou Son of God? art thou come hither to torment us before the time?" (Matt. 8:28, 29).

"And, behold, a woman of Canaan came out of the same coasts, and cried unto him, saying, Have mercy on me, O Lord, thou son of David; my daughter is grievously vexed with a devil" (Matt. 15:22).

"And, behold, a man of the company cried out, saying, Master, I beseech thee, look upon my son; for he is mine only child. And, lo, a spirit taketh him, and he suddenly crieth out; and it teareth him that he foameth again, and bruising him, hardly departeth from him. And as he was yet a coming, the devil threw him down, and tare him. And Jesus rebuked the unclean spirit, and healed the child, and delivered him again to his father" (Luke 9:38, 39, 42).

"And when he had called unto him his twelve disciples, he gave them power against unclean spirits, to cast them out, and to heal all manner of sickness and all manner of disease" (Matt. 10:1).

"And the seventy returned again with joy, saying, Lord, even the devils are subject unto us through thy name" (Luke 10:17).

"What say I then? that the idol is any thing, or that which is offered in sacrifice to idols is any thing? But I say, that the things which the Gentiles sacrifice, they sacrifice to devils, and not to God: and I would not that ye should have fellowship with devils. Ye cannot drink the cup of the Lord, and the cup of devils: ye cannot be partakers of the Lord's table, and of the table of devils" (I Cor. 10:19-21).

"For such are false apostles, deceitful workers, transforming themselves into the apostles of Christ. And no marvel; for Satan himself is transformed into an angel of light. Therefore it is no great thing if his ministers also be transformed as the minister of righteousness; whose end shall be according to their works" (II Cor. 11: 13-15).

WHAT DO YOU SAY?

1. Why are there seemingly more cases of demon possession in more superstitious cultures? Does this mean the demons do not or cannot possess people in so-called cultured countries? Does the intellectual capacity of a person determine whether he can be possessed by a demon?

2. Can we identify modern counterparts of the demonic possession described in the New Testament? Were those manifestations simply allowed to show the divinity of Christ and the power of the gospel in the early church?

3. If demonism is real today, why don't we have more discernable examples? Are such examples non-existent, or do they simply go unrecognized? Can they be recognized without rejecting the discoveries of modern psychological research?

4. Is there any relationship between demonism and the current interest in occultism, astrology, spiritualism, psychic phenomena?

5. Are there any instances of demonism in Scripture that could legitimately be described in psychological terminology? Give examples.

6. Have phenomena commonly attributed to evil spirits been shown to be results of abnormal psychological factors within the human personality?

7. Is it possible that some ailments now described as emotional disturbances are actually caused or aggravated by demon possession? Can demon possession be helped by psychiatry?

8. Can the church use the valuable knowledge gained in recent years in the field of psychiatry as a weapon to fight cases of demon possession? Can the

Holy Spirit use these techniques in cases of demon possession?

9. If, after "trying the spirits" according to I John 4:1, we believe a person is demon possessed or demon influenced, what should we do for that person? What dangers are involved?

10. Is it possible that churches have so lost their powers of discernment that Christians cannot recognize cases of demonic posession? How can we regain such discernment?

11. Is there any relationship between the rising evidence of demonism and the expansion of Satanic power before the Second Coming of Christ? Are there any specific scriptural references?

Notes

1. Arthur Johnston, "Encounter with a Parisian Sorceress," *Horizons,* Jan.-Feb. 1968. Used by permission.

2. Marilyn Hoyt, "The Witch Doctor Said 'Kill,' " *Horizons,* Mar.-Apr. 1968. Used by permission.

3. Russel T. Hitt, "Demons Today," *Eternity,* May 1969. Used by permission.

4. Ray B. Buker, Sr., "Are Demons Real Today?" *Christian Life,* March 1968. Used by permission of Christian Life Publications, Inc., Gunderson Drive and Schmale Road, Wheaton, Illinois 60187.

More Leisure – How Should We Use It? 12

LEISURE HAS BEEN CITED as one of the three modern dangers that face our civilization; the other two being nuclear war and overpopulation. Man seems less prepared to cope with the potential of more leisure than he is with most of his other problems. Having more leisure sneaks up on man so fast that the reaction often has been to fill free time with meaningless activities. It doesn't seem important what a man is doing as long as he keeps occupied. Idleness has usually been considered sin in our society. Work has usually been considered virtuous. In the process, however, man seems to have confused work with busyness, idleness with relaxation, and pleasure with leisure.

Since the beginning of the 19th century, Americans have reduced their work week from about 70 hours to less than 40. Yet they act as if they have less leisure time than their forefathers. They do not seem to know how to really enjoy their time. In spite of modern conveniences that free man from many of his burdens, much of his so-called "free" time is frittered away in traffic congestion, commuting on trains, waiting in grocery lines, being part of crowds in department stores, moonlighting, watching meaningless or mediocre TV programs, and repairing cars, appliances and houses. Man spends less time gathering food and hunting than did people in primitive

120

societies, but now he has a host of other "necessities" that eat up his time. He has more goods and services to make his life easier and less hectic, yet lives a more hectic one than ever before. No matter what a man's socioeconomic level, he is still plagued by what is commonly called the "rat race." People have become slaves to their possessions and the endless activities that fill their free time.

Man's unpreparedness to properly use leisure time results in the obvious boredom that plagues modern man. Too many people have "time on their hands." Others seek ways to "kill time." Unless they "have something to do" they become frustrated and anxious. Like the preacher in Ecclesiastes they find life a "vexation" of the spirit since "nothing is new under the sun." Such people look upon time in terms of quantity — so many hours in which to do a specific number of activities. How can they fill up their days? Few take a qualitative look — what significant, beneficial, rewarding and constructive things can be done?

U. S. News & World Report recently called leisure the "fastest-growing business in America." The leisure business comes to over $83 billion — more money than is spent annually for national defense. Leisure time activities have become big business. For such things as boats, color TV's, camping equipment, Americans spend more than $38 billion. This is up 11.4 percent from 1965. Americans will spend close to $40 billion on traveling in this country in 1970. This includes food, lodging, transportation, and other entertainment expenses. *U. S. News & World Report* calls this "an astonishing picture of America at play."

A key word in the American use of leisure is "activity." Americans like to travel and see things. They like to be doing something. And our affluent society makes it possible to see almost anything and do almost anything one wishes. Leisure is pleasure and pleasure is leisure, and perhaps too many people look at their free time only in this narrow sense. It is not wrong to have fun or enjoy life; this is a natural fruit of good living and an assumed privilege in Scripture (Eccl. 2:24-26; I Cor. 3:21-23).

The Christian, however, has a different attitude toward leisure and pleasure than the non-Christian. Webster defines leisure as, "free time from the demands of work" and "freedom to do something." But it is not a freedom apart from responsibility. For the Christian, his time as well as his money is part of his stewardship. Leisure is not an adjunct to his Christian life and faith. His time is never separated from his faith. Yet, for some, religion is something to be pursued only during their leisure time. The true Christian makes no separation between leisure and other time — he is accountable to God for every moment of his life.

"Whether a Christian uses his leisure for playing a musical instrument, painting pictures, reading adventure stories, gardening, mountain climbing, bowling, or any one of a thousand other things is an optional matter. God has given us a host of pursuits richly to enjoy. The scriptural criterion of what we may do is unequivocally stated by St. Paul in Colossians 3:17, 'And whatsoever you do in word or deed, do all in the name of the Lord Jesus, giving thanks to God and the Father by him.' But religion (using the word in the high sense of the practice of Christianity) is not for the believer an elective, spare time pursuit like going to football games or bird watching. It is life itself, and it comprehends everything Christians do and say and hear and think. To be sure, certain practices of religion, such as attendance at church, reading the Bible, visiting the sick, and helping the underprivileged, are done in the time apart from the daily job. Yet the claims of Jesus Christ are all-inclusive. Nothing is ever irrelevant to him with whom we have to do.

"Christ is the Lord of time — of free time as well as of working time. Those who are His are responsible for the stewardship of the time He gives them. One of the great New Testament phrases is the twice repeated one of the Apostle, 'redeeming the time' (Eph. 5:16; Col. 4:5). Our Lord Himself lived under the pressing stewardship of time, as we know from His reiterated 'Mine hour is not yet come' . . . We are accountable for the stewardship of our leisure as well as our working time. From the daily work there is indeed leisure, but from the unremitting exercise of Christian responsibility there is no such thing as spare time. No Christian is ever off-duty from God. Leisure and working time are equally to be accounted for to the Lord who said, 'Lift up your eyes, and look on the fields; for they are white already to harvest' (John 4:35)."[1]

A common misconception among Christians is that they must always be busy "producing" and "working." The more active they are the more "spiritual" they think themselves to be. Mr. David Ewert, writing in *The Voice*, says, "people who can hold down two jobs, who can work 16 hours a day — preferably with brawn, rather than with brain — who can get by with little sleep, who never take a holiday, who have 'drive,' who can 'produce,' are the saintlier sons of God. Instead of admitting that they are enslaved, frequently to the mighty dollar, or to the taskmaster, prestige, and so are driven to the limit of their resources, they might piously claim to be 'redeeming the time.'

"It should be pointed out, however, that although God's Word condemns idleness, there is a subtle danger in the attitude just described. In it lies the denial of the religious value of the contemplative life. Moreover, some dear souls feel extremely guilty when they do not fill up their week with 'rewarding' (usually that means money) work, lest they be judged for not redeeming their time. Others are simply afraid to enjoy the luxury of leisure, lest they fall behind in the chase for 'things' which the proverbial Joneses have, and so they 'redeem the time,' and do not realize that their lives are being cluttered up with many 'things.' Clearly, we are in need of some biblical perspectives from which to look at leisure.

"Leisure, for the Christian, cannot be merely left-over time: it is too important and too serious to be so lightly regarded. But it does not follow that when he fills up time with a maddening succession of activity that he is redeeming the time."[2]

What will man do with his leisure time as it expands? Will the freedom from endless labor release him from the insecurities and fears that now separate mankind? Will man know how to use his leisure to pursue peace and goodness? Or will man simply have more time to perfect the means of warfare? Will he pursue what most benefits all men or just those things that please the privileged few? What will the men of leisure do in the future — serve the public or satisfy the pampered? Now is certainly the time to think about what to do with the freedoms produced by our automated age, as day by day man possesses more hours in which to decide for himself how he will spend his time.

WHAT DOES THE BIBLE SAY?

"And on the seventh day God ended his work which he had made; and he rested on the seventh day from all his work which he had made" (Gen. 2:2).

"My times are in thy hand; deliver me from the hand of mine enemies, and from them that persecute me" (Ps. 31:15).

"He maketh me to lie down in green pastures: he leadeth me beside the still waters. He restoreth my soul: he leadeth me in the paths of righteousness for his name's sake" (Ps. 23:2, 3).

"And they say, 'How can God know? Is there knowledge in the Most High?' Behold, these are the wicked; always at ease, they increase in riches" (Ps. 73:11, 12; RSV).

"But the wicked are like the troubled sea, when it cannot rest, whose waters cast up mire and dirt. There is no peace, saith my God, to the wicked" (Isa. 57:20, 21).

"Come unto me, all ye that labor and are heavy laden, and I will give you rest. Take my yoke upon you, and learn of me; for I am meek and lowly in heart: and ye shall find rest unto your souls" (Matt. 11:28, 29).

"And he said unto them, Come ye yourselves apart into a desert place, and rest a while: for there were many coming and going, and they had no leisure so much as to eat" (Mark 6:31).

"And Jesus answered and said unto her, Martha, Martha, thou art careful and troubled about many things. But one thing is needful; and Mary hath chosen that good part, which shall not be taken away from her" (Luke 10:41, 42).

"And I will say to my soul, Soul, thou hast much goods laid up for many years; take thine ease, eat, drink and be merry" (Luke 12:19).

"See then that ye walk circumspectly, not as fools, but as wise, Redeeming the time, because the days are evil" (Eph. 5:15, 16).

"Walk in wisdom toward them that are without, redeeming the time" (Col. 4:5).

"There is nothing better for a man, than that he should eat and drink, and that he should make his soul enjoy good in his labor. This also I saw, that it was from the hand of God" (Eccl. 2:24).

WHAT DO YOU SAY?

1. What is the difference between leisure and idleness? Does leisure imply absence of work? Does it always imply pleasure or rest?

2. In what ways is modern man unprepared for increased free time? Why has more free time produced boredom for many people? How is boredom related to a person's inner life?

3. What is the meaning of the scriptural admonition to "redeem the time" (Eph. 5:16)? Why is the use of time given such great emphasis in the New Testament?

4. What has contributed to the common misconception that Christians must always be "producing" and "contributing?" Does constant activity imply spirituality? Why or why not?

5. What are the dangers of constant activity without taking time out for leisure and rest? Is there anything wrong in taking it easy to enjoy whatever one pleases?

6. Has the increase of leisure time affected church attendance and church activities? What can be done about the tendency of Christians to use Sunday as a day for leisurely activities away from church?

7. What affect would the proposed three-day-weekends have on Sunday church activities? In what ways would such weekends give the church more opportunities for service and witness? How would

churches have to change their program? Could they leave them as they are?

8. How has the American "rat race" influenced Christians and their use of leisure? What are the dangers of equating leisure primarily with pleasure?

9. Give some examples of good uses of leisure time. What are some poor uses? Can the use made of leisure time distinguish Christians from unbelievers? How?

10. What picture do we get in the New Testament of Jesus' use of time? What was His attitude toward leisure (cf. Mark 6:31)? Did Jesus seem hurried or rushed?

11. How should Christians use their vacation time? How can vacations become more profitable — spiritually, mentally, physically?

Notes

1. "The Christian Use of Leisure," *Christianity Today*, January 31, 1964. Copyright 1964 by *Christianity Today*. Reprinted by permission.

2. David Ewert, "The Christian Use of Leisure," *The Voice*. Used by permission.

Are "Christian" Funerals Christian? 13

Most Christians make adequate eternal preparation for death. Faith in Jesus Christ is the assurance of heaven. Fewer seem to make adequate preparation for the days, weeks or months they have to live while knowing a terminal date is nearing. Still fewer make adequate preparation for disposing of their bodies after death.

To make funeral preparations while in sound body and in sound mind seems ridiculous. In fact, some would accuse their relatives of wanting to get rid of them if arrangements were finalized beforehand with a funeral director. Others firmly believe that funeral preparations are best made at the time of death. A certain amount of grief, inconvenience, and hardship shows how much the deceased was appreciated and loved.

Others do not make adequate funeral arrangements simply because of the human desire to live. No one really thinks he is going to die. Thus the majority of Christians, like non-Christians, do not visit a funeral director to specify what kind of funeral they want. Like non-Christians, most Christians simply accept (either consciously or by default) the traditional funeral practices of our American culture.

To show respect for the deceased, the average family pays over $1500 in funeral costs. Friends and relatives awkwardly seek to express words of comfort while viewing the body. Funeral services often include hollow eulogies and rather morbid music, and the graveside committal becomes somewhat of an anticlimactic last show for those who attend the funeral. Is this the Christian approach?

Dr. Bruce R. Reichenbach, assistant professor of philosophy at Augsburg College, Minneapolis, tells his personal experience at his grandmother's death — and his reactions to a typical "Christian" funeral:

"There she lay, snuggled in satin, the soft, pink kind she could never afford to enjoy while she was alive. And the casket, a gleaming, decorated bronze one, was shiny and new. When did she last have something so shiny and new to catch her fascinated gaze? Five, ten years ago? We gave her a lovely, expensive coffin and a poverty-stricken existence. We were generous with the money for the tombstone — indeed it cost more than all of the last three Christmas gifts combined. She has luxury now — but she's dead and cannot know.

"Few ever deferred to her when she was alive. Yet in the funeral parlor the voices that once argued with her and shouted her down scarcely reached a whisper. The highest pitch was the sickly soft of the electric organ. . . .

"Were not our values awry? Was not this truly a 'transvaluation of values'? The conduct of deference (selfishness), of giving for the sake of another's comfort, of reverence, was performed in painstakingly perfect pageantry for the dead, not for the living. For her unfeeling 'comfort' we generously offered her the finest, smoothest satin; for her fitful, uneasy sleep, lumps for a mattress and old cold sheets for covers. For her corpsely rest we gave her shiny brass; for her unselfish love, trinkets of tinsel, the little Christmas check to salve our conscience. To her stiffened face we deferred in silence; behind her living back we gossipped. A transvaluation of values indeed!

"Then there was the funeral sermon. The minister, dressed in black, himself seemingly broken, slowly rose to euologize her. What wonderful words of tribute to this woman — a woman he never knew. What praise bestowed — on a person to whom he had never spoken. . . . How irreverent for the stranger to comfort the estranged with the same generalities he used at his last funeral. Are we all platitudinously alike?"[1]

A man who lived next door to a funeral home, Dr. Burton H. Throckmorton, Jr., Hayes Professor of New Testament at Bangor (Me.) Theological Seminary, says that our primitive ideas about death are the cause of many of our funeral practices. He especially feels that body viewing comes out of a mystical feeling that the living can somehow identify with the dead. He says:

"I have known devout Christians to spend hours standing by a casket, looking fondly at the body of a loved one, obviously believing that by so doing they were placing themselves in communion with one who only ostensibly had died. One understands the enormous pressures that come into play at such a time, the deep desire to maintain contact, to deny that separation is absolute. But it is doubtful that those who grieve should be encouraged to place their faith in an illusion.

"As the grieving survivor takes his last look at the body when the casket top is lowered, it is often obvious that he feels that at that moment he is losing contact forever with the person he has loved. The committal service at graveside can be terrifying to those who mourn, since they have associated a kind of quasi-life with the corpse, have felt that it provides them with a means of communication now to be ended.

"Facilitating the inability of the mourners to come to terms with the reality of death is the work of 'beautification' performed by the mortician. If one looks on a badly mangled body one tends to be repulsed by it, to be driven away from it; he realizes that what he sees is not the person he has known. But when one visits the funeral home and looks on a body that has been restored, painted, dressed up, made to look 'natural' and 'lifelike' he is not repulsed but attracted. Attracted to what? Not, surely, to a carcass, to what remains after life has ceased, but — so he thinks — to the person who still *is*.

"While it is probably true that the mortician's work facilitates the primitive notion that the person is somehow to be associated with the corpse, we must not put all the blame on the men in black suits. They may capitalize on the belief that the dead aren't really dead, but they didn't initiate the belief, and they are not the only ones who perpetuate the impression that some element of the person is still united in a mysterious way with the object that lies in the casket. . . .

"If death were taken with real seriousness the corpse would have far less magnetic power than it so often exercises. The demand for an 'open casket' at the funeral service is certainly related to belief that the person for whom the service is conducted is actually present. Hence the 'person' becomes the center of the service; his casket is placed in the most prominent spot."[2]

Beside the selection of casket flowers, and funeral service arrangements, is the selection of a burial site and the necessary (or suggested) vault, etc. To take away the stigma of death, burial places have been renamed "memorial gardens," "rest parks," etc. Many modern cemeteries do not allow tombstones, only grave markers. Lawns are kept perpetually green and trimmed. Soft music can be heard throughout the "gardens" from the central chapel, and the gardens are sectioned off into "parks."

One vault manufacturer states that a burial vault

symbolizes the family's tribute and devotion to the deceased for all the years to come. Such a vault is declared to be both sensible and economical to provide indefinite protection for the casket and its contents.

The emphasis upon the body and the respect paid to it has minimized any emphasis on cremation. This practice, widely practiced in other parts of the world — especially the Orient — has never taken hold in the American culture. In fact, there's considerable campaigning against cremation, which especially has been frowned on by the church.

Faris D. Whitesell, Professor Emeritus of Pastoral Theology at Northern Baptist Seminary, Oakbrook, Ill., gives the following suggestions to pastors who attempt to Christianize "Christian" funerals. Laymen can profit from these suggestions:

"The man of God should make his funerals as Christian as possible. Quite a few relics of heathenism survive in some of our funeral practices. He will avoid these, for the minister is supposed to Christianize everything he does.

"The pastor should consult with the family about the expenditures for the funeral. He can tactfully guide them away from unnecessary expense for clothing, casket, vault, funeral cars, and elaborate floral displays. He can show that these put undue emphasis on the corpse. The redeemed personality had gone to be with the Lord, and wasteful expense on the body is unchristian.

"The funeral service itself should be simple, scriptural, comforting, and short. The pastor will talk directly to the living, not orate about the dead.

"He will not try to arouse emotion. Grief has its rightful place in mourning and should not be rigidly suppressed, but excessive emotional display at a funeral is heathenish. The pastor will speak to comfort, heal, encourage, and enlighten.

"The practice of having the casket closed just before the funeral service promotes the Christian emphasis. There seems to be something heathenish in having people parade around the casket for a final look at the corpse after the funeral service has ended. Often there may be excessive weeping, wailing, and even emotional collapse, as mourners touch the body or kiss it, or maybe embrace it in a final farewell. If the casket has been closed before the service begins, such scenes are avoided.

"After all, the corpse is not the departed, and no affection lavished on it can help the deceased. The body is to be revered only as the house in which the departed lived and as its link with the resurrection body of glory and power, like unto Christ's glorified resurrection body.

"The interment service at the grave would be more Christian if it were attended only by the relatives. A curious crowd of outsiders looking on may please the bereaved family and seem like a show of respect for the departed, but it is an overemphasis on the body."[3]

WHAT DOES THE BIBLE SAY?

"And they buried him in his own sepulchres, which he had made for himself in the city of David, and laid him in the bed which was filled with sweet odors and divers kinds of spices prepared by the apothecaries' art: and they made a very great burning for him" (II Chron. 16:14).

"And David said to Joab, and to all the people that were with him, Rend your clothes, and gird you with sackcloth, and mourn before Abner. And king David himself followed the bier. And they buried Abner in Hebron: and the King lifted up his voice, and wept at the grave of Abner; and all the people wept" (II Sam. 3:31, 32).

"And Joseph fell upon his father's face, and wept upon him, and kissed him. And Joseph commanded his servants the physicians to embalm his father: and the physicians embalmed Israel. And forty days were fulfilled for him; for so are fulfilled the days of those which are embalmed: and the Egyptians mourned for him three score and ten days. . . . My father made me swear, saying, Lo, I die: in my grave which I have digged for me in the land of Canaan, there shalt thou bury me. . . . And Joseph went up to bury his father: and with him went up all the servants of Pharaoh, the elders of his house, and all the elders of the land of Egypt, And all the house of Joseph, and his brethren, and his father's house . . ." (Gen. 50:1-3, 5, 7, 8).

"And Joseph took an oath of the children of Israel, saying, God will surely visit you, and ye shall carry up my bones from hence. So Joseph died, being a hundred and ten years old: and they embalmed him, and he was put in a coffin in Egypt" (Gen. 50:25).

"And the women also, which came with him from Galilee, followed after, and beheld the sepulchre, and how his body was laid. And they returned, and prepared spices and ointments, and rested the sabbath day according to the commandment" (Luke 23:55, 56).

"Now in the place where he was crucified there was a garden; and in the garden a new sepulchre, wherein was never man yet laid. There laid they Jesus therefore because of the Jews' preparation day; for the sepulchre was nigh at hand" (John 19:41, 42).

"So they went, and made the sepulchre sure, sealing the stone . . ." (Matt. 27:66).

"And whosoever toucheth one that is slain with a sword in the open fields, or a dead body, or a bone of a man, or a grave, shall be unclean seven days" (Num. 19:16).

"All the valiant men arose, and went all night, and took the body of Saul and the bodies of his sons from the wall of Bethshan, and came to Jabesh, and burnt them there. And they took their bones, and buried them under a tree . . ." (I Sam. 31:12, 13).

WHAT DO YOU SAY?

1. Is our assumption that traditional funeral practices show respect for the dead a valid one?

2. Should Christians reverse the practices of expensive, rather morbid funeral arrangements? If so, how?

3. Why do people hesitate to make pre-death funeral arrangements?

4. Why hasn't cremation become popular in the Christian world? Is cremation unchristian?

5. If Christians believe that the body is only the house in which a person dwells while upon earth, why is so much emphasis put on preserving it after death?

6. Does a person have a right to decide how he will be buried? How can you be assured that your concepts of burial will be followed by your loved ones when you die?

7. Would a private burial without a showing of the body, followed by a church memorial service, better proclaim the Christian view of death? Why? or why not?

8. What significance, if any, do Christ's words, "Let the dead bury their dead" (Luke 9:60) have in relation to today's funeral practices?

9. What type of funeral sermon ought a pastor preach at a funeral where the dead person was a believer? was an unbeliever? Should eulogies be eliminated? Why?

10. Since conducting funerals is big business, subject to abuse, what standards can be set up by outside agencies, such as the church, to protect those whose grief might be exploited?

11. Is there a burial association in your area? What are its purposes? advantages? What is the procedure for joining? Should churches organize such associations?

Notes

1. Bruce R. Reichenbach, "Grandma's Funeral: Painful Post-Mortem," *Eternity*, October 1969. Used by permission.

2. Burton H. Throckmorton, Jr., "Do Christians Believe in Death?" *The Christian Century*, May 21, 1969. Copyright 1969 Christian Century Foundation. Reprinted by permission from the May 21, 1969 issue of *The Christian Century*.

3. Faris D. Whitesell, "Ten Ways to Christianize Funerals," *Sunday School Times and Gospel Herald*, July 1, 1969. Reprinted by permission of Union Gospel Press, Cleveland, Ohio.